Butterflies
of South West Scotland

An Atlas of their distribution

Keith Futter, Richard Sutcliffe, David Welham, Anne Welham,
A. John Rostron, Jessie MacKay, Neil Gregory, Jim McCleary,
T. Norman Tait, Jim Black and Paul Kirkland

ARGYLL✤PUBLISHING

This book is dedicated to the late
Bill Brackenridge,
a former committee member of
the Glasgow & South West
Scotland branch
of Butterfly Conservation,
who tragically died as a result of a
car accident in 2000

Argyll Publishing
Glendaruel
Argyll PA22 3AE
www.argyllpublishing.com

**British Library Cataloguing-in-Publication
Data.**
**A catalogue record for this book is available
from the British Library.**

ISBN 1 902831 95 0

Printing & Binding
Cromwell Press Ltd, Wiltshire

We gratefully acknowledge the financial
support in producing this book provided by:

The National Lottery Awards for All;
Scottish Natural Heritage;
Blodwen Lloyd Binns Bequest Fund
(administered by the Glasgow Natural
History Society);
Royal Bank of Scotland Community
Cashback Scheme;
Butterfly Conservation (Glasgow & South
West Scotland branch).

Proceeds from the sale of this book will
help Butterfly Conservation.

Contents

Dark Green Fritillary

Foreword

There has never been more interest in Scottish butterflies, these 'living jewels' that enliven our countryside walks, grace our gardens and parks, and, often in the form of caterpillars, that can initiate in children a fascination with the natural world that lasts a lifetime.

It is very pleasing that this increasing interest has led to a great surge of activity in recording, monitoring and practical habitat management work. The credit for this high profile must go to the many hundreds of enthusiastic volunteers of all ages who give so freely of their time.

Butterflies (and moths) in Scotland have had very mixed fortunes in recent years but most of us realise that we now see far fewer butterflies on our country walks than we used to. Loss of wild habitats, intensification of agriculture, drainage of wetlands, and afforestation with alien conifers have all resulted in huge declines. Climate change is also having its effect, and so it is perhaps not surprising that the distribution of many of our butterflies is changing rapidly.

In fact, butterflies can serve as excellent indicators of the health of our countryside, something promoted by Butterfly Conservation Scotland in its work with the public, volunteers, landowners and policy makers. Many species are very sensitive to changes in habitat and the condition of their foodplants, and most are also very dependent on sunshine, temperature and humidity. Moreover, several of our most threatened species seem to need large areas of habitat – small nature reserves are just not sufficient in the long-term. Thus when things start going wrong, it is butterflies that are one of the first groups to disappear, and recent research has shown that they have been declining far more quickly than birds or plants.

However, on a more positive note, when things are going right, butterflies can rapidly increase and spread, and we hope that as farming and forestry becomes more 'wildlife-friendly' we will begin to see widespread improvements in their fortunes.

Recording the changes in the distribution and abundance of our butterflies is thus crucial, showing us which species are increasing and which species are in need of more conservation effort. In this way, every single butterfly record assists us to focus our conservation work.

With impeccable timing, the Glasgow and South West Scotland Branch have produced an absorbing book that makes full use of the upsurge in recording over the last ten years. Not least, we hope this book provides invaluable feedback to all those who have submitted records to Butterfly Conservation, local record centres and others. The records themselves are now readily available to all via the National Biodiversity Network (www.nbn.org.uk).

So, on behalf of Butterfly Conservation Scotland, many thanks indeed to all of you who have contributed records, and thereby helped to conserve butterflies in the region. Special thanks must go to Richard Sutcliffe who has co-ordinated the recording in the region over many years, and to Dr Keith Futter who spotted the opportunity to produce this book, and most importantly, has achieved it.

So, please help us with our recording and conservation work, but above all, enjoy this book!

Paul Kirkland
Director, Butterfly Conservation
Scotland
December 2005

Green Hairstreak – butterflies are living jewels that can enhance our daily lives by their beauty

Introduction
Why produce an Atlas?

The purpose of this book is to summarise the distribution of butterflies found in South West Scotland and present an analysis of their current status. Conducting a detailed survey of butterflies and producing an atlas of their distribution is the first step to understand the state of butterfly populations and identify trends. Conservation measures, monitoring and research can then be targeted at those species in decline.

In 1980 George Thomson produced the landmark publication, *The Butterflies of Scotland,* which provided a summary of the distribution of butterflies and historical records in Scotland. In 1985 the Glasgow and South West Scotland branch of Butterfly Conservation was founded. Butterfly Conservation is a charity dedicated to saving butterflies and moths and their habitats. It has over thirty branches covering the whole of the UK. Since its foundation the Glasgow branch, with Richard Sutcliffe at the helm as either Chairman or Recorder, has been co-ordinating the recording of butterflies and their distribution in South West Scotland. The data that has been collected is both impressive in terms of the number of records analysed and by the area covered.

A male Northern Brown Argus, also known as the Scottish White Spot

The Glasgow branch provided detailed records of butterfly distributions in South West Scotland for the publication, *Millennium Atlas of Butterflies in Britain and Ireland* (Asher *et al.* 2001), which covered the five year period 1995-99. Comprehensive recording of butterflies also continued during the following five years 2000-2004. As a branch we now have a comprehensive set of data covering the ten year period from 1995-2004. It is this detailed data set that we have used to produce the maps presented in this atlas. By comparing the first five year recording period with the second five years we can also establish which butterflies are doing well and which are not.

This book is not intended to be an identification guide. However, in addition to presenting distribution maps, we have also included photographs of each species and a commentary on their identification, life cycle, distribution and abundance. There are also some observations that we believe may not have been previously published.

Why Do We Record Butterflies and their Distribution?

As a branch of Butterfly Conservation we feel that conserving butterflies and their habitats is important to stimulate interest in butterflies and natural history in general. Many people, especially children, like butterflies. Indeed butterfly watching is becoming an increasingly popular pastime. Many take the time to observe the butterflies where they live and pass this information to recording centres.

The results obtained from recording the distribution of butterflies can serve a valuable function as an environmental indicator. As an environmental issue, climate change and global warming in particular, is being discussed more frequently. Some take the issue seriously, others not so, some are even dismissive. As sun worshippers, butterflies and many of their caterpillars are very sensitive to variations in temperature. They are very good indicators of changes in climate and their distribution can provide clues to the state of the environment. This atlas clearly shows that for some butterflies their distributions are changing. These changes may well be linked to alterations in our climate.

This atlas has been compiled to promote butterfly conservation and to commemorate the twentieth anniversary of the Glasgow and South West Scotland branch of Butterfly Conservation. It has also been produced as an acknowledge-ment to the efforts made by a large number of volunteers who have contributed records of butterflies found in our branch area, as without those records this publication would not have been possible. This book has been a team effort with all branch committee members being involved together with Paul Kirkland, the Director of Butterfly Conservation in Scotland. Valuable contributions have also been made from members of the branch, in particular T. Norman Tait and Dr Jim Black.

Area Covered and Diversity of Habitats

The Glasgow and South West Scotland branch of Butterfly Conservation covers the general regions of Dumfries & Galloway, Ayrshire, Greater Glasgow, Stirlingshire, Argyll and the Isles, Dunbartonshire and Loch Lomond. The political boundaries changed in 1996, largely due to the dissolution of Strathclyde as a region. The Watsonian vice-counties remain a useful constant and our branch area covers 13 vice-counties (Kinnear & Kirkland 2000). To provide continuity in an often changing political landscape we have chosen to adopt the vice-counties as a descriptive area for this atlas. The true boundary of the Glasgow and South West Scotland branch, which is similar to the vice county boundaries, with minor modifications, was established at the 'Treaty of Kindrogan' 1996, to separate the three branches in Scotland (see history of the branch, page 14).

The diverse geology of South West Scotland supports a variety of habitats

Richard Sutcliffe (left), with Andrew Phillips, previous Director of Butterfly Conservation, (centre) and Dr Eric Watson (right) at Blackhill Mire, Helensburgh. Richard has co-ordinated the recording of butterflies in South West Scotland since 1985

Map of Vice Counties of South West Scotland

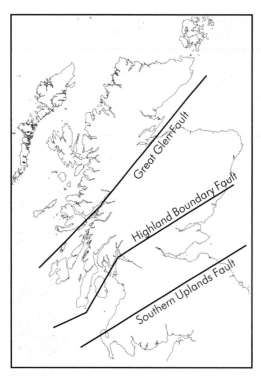
Schematic map of geological faults

with other sedimentary rocks and Carboniferous volcanic rocks. The Southern Uplands comprise large stretches of sedimentary rocks including greywacke, shales and New Red Sandstone surrounding outcrops of volcanic granites. The soils above the metamorphic, volcanic and sandstone rocks usually range from neutral to acid with alkaline soils being rare and generally restricted to coastal areas due to shell-rich deposits or local outcrops of limestone.

Geology can exert a strong influence on butterfly distributions. A good example is the Highland Boundary Fault in Dunbartonshire which has a dramatic effect on the distribution of the Scotch Argus. North of the fault the Scotch Argus is widespread and locally abundant but south of the fault it is absent from much of southern Scotland until it re-occurs either side of the Southern Uplands fault in Ayrshire and Dumfries & Galloway.

and landscapes that affect butterfly distributions. Three major geological faults occur, the Great Glen Fault, the Highland Boundary Fault and the Southern Uplands Fault. The Great Glen Fault marks the north west boundary of our branch. The Highland Boundary Fault, cutting through Loch Lomond and Arran, marks the transition between the Highland and Lowland scenery until the Southern Uplands Fault in Dumfries & Galloway provides a further area of mountainous terrain.

Between the Great Glen Fault and the Highland Boundary Fault the geology is dominated by Dalradian rocks, predominantly metamorphic schists interspersed with granites. South of the Highland Boundary Fault to the Southern Uplands deposits of Devonian old red sandstone and Carboniferous sandstones, coals, and limestones, occur

Agriculture in South West Scotland is predominantly pastoral, with sheep grazing dominant. There are also locally important areas for herds of dairy cattle. Much lowland agricultural land has been 'improved' and provides poor habitats for butterflies as modern varieties of grass have replaced wildflower-rich native grassland. Upland grasslands are generally poor for butterflies due to climatic conditions and heavy grazing by sheep.

The South West Scotland area is one of the few places in Britain which has intact peat bog habitats, indeed Flanders Moss near Stirling is the largest intact, lowland raised bog in the UK. These peatlands support Large Heaths, Small Heaths and Green Hairstreaks. Many of

Small Pearl-bordered Fritillary, a butterfly that has declined over much of its range in England and Wales, is locally common in SW Scotland

the bog habitats have unfortunately been damaged by drainage and poor land management and they remain one of the most threatened habitats in South West Scotland.

Woodlands can be variable in quality with the many coniferous plantations being generally poor habitats for butterflies. A greater butterfly diversity can be found at ancient woodlands, for example along the Clyde Valley, at Loch Lomondside and at the native or diverse woodlands found in Argyll, and in Dumfries & Galloway. The best woodlands support Pearl-bordered Fritillary, Small Pearl-bordered Fritillary, Speckled Wood, Ringlet and Purple Hairstreak.

The greatest floral diversity in South West Scotland is usually found along the coastal fringe or when the underlying geology provides a variety of soil types, or where mineral rich flushing occurs. At these areas of high floral diversity the greatest number of butterflies is usually observed. Species such as Common Blue, Small Copper, Large Skipper, Northern Brown Argus, Dark Green Fritillary, Wall Brown and Grayling are most common at the coastal fringe. The coastline of Argyll and the island network have a warm and wet climate with the Gulf Stream producing an important warming effect in the winter. The locally warmer climate may allow the Chequered Skipper and Marsh Fritillary to thrive in parts of Argyll.

Although South West Scotland has a high proportion of open countryside, the Greater Glasgow region, with approximately one million people, is at

The Common Blue is a butterfly most frequently seen along the coast but it has also successfully colonised urban waste ground

the heart of the area and has an impact on butterfly populations. The large urban area of Glasgow together with the peripheral towns can attract butterflies to the extent that for some species such as the Peacock, Small Tortoiseshell, Small White and Large White, one is more likely to see these butterflies in a garden than in the wider countryside. Undeveloped waste ground often supports Buddleia and town gardens offer rich nectaring sites, particularly for the migrant species such as Red Admiral, Painted Lady and Clouded Yellow. The Grayling, Common Blue and Small Copper have also been successful in occupying some of the waste ground in Glasgow and industrial areas in Ayrshire.

Despite some very high quality habitats and large areas of open countryside found in South West Scotland it is the climate that is one of the main factors affecting butterfly distributions and abundance. The high rainfall and cooler temperatures of South West Scotland compared with, for example, southern England means that butterfly abundance and species diversity is relatively low. Whereas twenty or more species could be seen at a site in Dorset or Hampshire on a single day, only a very few sites in South West Scotland can boast twenty species in a year! Indeed, you would be doing well to see more than five species on a day visit to a site in South West Scotland and ten species would be exceptional.

Butterfly Conservation Scotland
Glasgow & South West Scotland Branch

The Glasgow & South West Scotland Branch of Butterfly Conservation (then known by its full name of The British Butterfly Conservation Society), was formed in 1985 and was the first branch to be established in Scotland.

Gerald (Gerry) Rodway was instrumental in forming the branch. He was in charge of the internationally important orchid collection in Glasgow Botanic Gardens, and a very competent photographer, who spent much of his spare time photographing butterflies and moths. He was a life member of the Society and was keen to establish a branch in Scotland.

There were then only about 30 members of the Society in the whole of Scotland. Gerry invited all those living in the west of Scotland, together with a few interested non-members he knew, to a meeting in his home at East Lodge, Botanic Gardens, Glasgow on 19 January 1985. Ten people turned up and unanimously agreed to form a branch. After some discussion it was agreed to call the branch the Glasgow and South West Scotland Branch. The branch area was to cover Strathclyde and Dumfries & Galloway Regions. This was partly because several members were particularly interested in, and often visited, the Solway coast.

The branch's initial aims were to conserve the Large Heath in the Greater Glasgow area and Mountain Ringlet on Ben Lomond; monitor the expansion of

Gerald Rodway, the founder of the Glasgow & South West Scotland branch of Butterfly Conservation

the Orange-tip; protection of habitats and establishment of new meadow land. There were to be field trips to record the distribution of butterflies in Galloway and study tours for beginners and children. It was also suggested to mount exhibits at the Dolphin Arts Centre in Bridgeton and have a display at the Glasgow Garden Festival in 1988, as well as give talks and lectures for education.

It was agreed to use the 'Scotch White Spot' (Northern Brown Argus) – one of the key species in Dumfries & Galloway, as the branch emblem. This led to the name of the branch newsletter 'On the Spot'.

Gerry Rodway was elected as the first chairman, but sadly he died unexpectedly in 1986, which was a major setback to the newly formed branch. Mike Kibby took over as chairman for a couple of years.

Initially most of the summer excursions were to visit known sites to see some of the rarer species. Most were to sites in Dumfries & Galloway, the Ayrshire coast and Argyll, but were occasionally further afield. Gerry introduced several members to the fabulous site at Whitbarrow Scar in Cumbria to see the Duke of Burgundy and there were a few visits to Angus and the Borders.

It wasn't long before the branch took an active role in local butterfly conservation. In 1985 the Ringlet was discovered at Cander Moss beside the M74 near Stonehouse – the first record for the species in Lanarkshire since 1911. Partly through members of the branch, the Scottish Wildlife Trust (SWT) were encouraged to take the site on as a reserve. In 1988 we established a butterfly transect at the site, which continues to this day.

For the first few years of its existence, the Glasgow and South West Scotland Branch was in effect the 'Scottish Branch'. This made it very difficult to organise events that were accessible to all members. It also meant that any queries to do with butterflies anywhere in Scotland were being channelled through the chairman, (from 1987), Richard Sutcliffe. Eventually Highland Branch was formed in 1993, and with the formation of East Scotland branch in 1995, the whole of Scotland was finally covered. At a meeting at Kindrogan Field Studies Centre in November 1996,

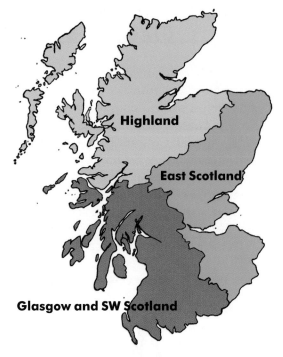

Scottish Butterfly Conservation branch boundaries declared by the Treaty of Kindrogan, 1996

representatives from all three Scottish branches agreed on definitive branch boundaries, based on Scottish Council boundaries. This was immediately declared the 'Treaty of Kindrogan' and was duly signed by the three branch chairmen.

A Regional Action Plan for the Glasgow and South West Scotland branch area was produced in December 2000 by Peter Kinnear and Paul Kirkland. This document aimed to target conservation action for threatened butterflies and moths in the branch area.

Not having a Butterfly Conservation Reserve in the area with which to get involved, members have instead helped with practical conservation at several SWT reserves over the years – helping with scrub clearance and similar activities.

Recording has always been an important and enjoyable activity of the branch.

As well as organising several excursions each summer, the branch also held two or three indoor meetings each winter. These were initially at Chatelherault Country Park, Hamilton but later mainly at Kelvingrove Museum, and more recently at the Botanic Gardens in Glasgow. On several occasions the speakers were actively involved in ground-breaking research on Scottish butterflies and moths, so members were kept up to date with the latest work which was taking place.

In the 1990s, committee member Neil McKenzie was elected to the National Executive of Butterfly Conservation. This was the first time that anyone from a Scottish branch had served on the Executive. Neil was able to make the point that Scotland needed more help from the National Society. As a result, Paul Kirkland was later appointed as the first paid member of staff of Butterfly Conservation to be based in Scotland, in 1996. Since then, Butterfly Conservation Scotland has established a noticeable presence in Scotland, based in Stirling, and currently employs 4 staff. More recently John Randall has served on the National Executive, representing Scotland.

One of our most active committee members, Bill Brackenridge, who worked as the Ecologist for North Lanarkshire Council was killed in a car accident in 2000. This left a major gap in the committee, as he was an active conservationist. This book is dedicated to his memory.

In 2004 Neil Gregory joined the branch committee and in 2005 set up the branch website at www.southwestscotland-butterflies.org.uk. This gives visitors to the site the chance to keep up to date with the latest branch news, find out what butterflies are currently on the wing and also allows them to send in records and observations.

Scrub clearance at Shewalton, Ayrshire to encourage butterflies at this Scottish Wildlife Trust Reserve.

Planting Birdsfoot-trefoil at Mugdock Country Park, north of Glasgow to enhance the habitat for Common Blue butterflies

Grayling caterpillar – a large colony of Graylings occurred at the site of the former steelworks at Ravenscraig, Motherwell. These gounds have since been built on but before the development of the site a survey was undertaken of the local area. As a last resort, in 1999, Grayling caterpillars were collected from parts of the site under threat by committee members, Richard Sutcliffe and Graham Irving and released at other suitable, adjacent locations in an attempt to facilitate the continuity of the colony

In the future there is likely to be a greater emphasis on the recording of moths, and the monitoring of butterflies that have experienced declines. The branch already runs several public moth nights each year, including a very popular one at the Botanic Gardens in Glasgow. Members are encouraged to record the moths they see, and submit them to the branch.

Of the ten 'founder members', three are still active members of the branch. Past and current committee members include Richard Sutcliffe, Dr Eric Watson, T. Norman Tait, Dr Michael Kibby, Anne Kibby, Jim Brockie, Dr David Barbour, Roy Henderson, Dr Gordon Sayer, Brenda Sayer, Dr Keith Futter, Jessie MacKay, Jim McCleary, Dr A. John Rostron, Neil McKenzie, Sue Agnew, Sue Wilkinson, Graham Irving, Prudence Williams, Dr Margaret Courtney, Bill Brackenridge, Tim Cook, David Welham, Anne Welham, and Neil Gregory. Richard Sutcliffe is the only founding member currently on the committee and has been a committee member for the entire duration of the history of the branch. In 1990 Keith Futter joined the branch and has been a committee member for fifteen years. In 2003 Keith Futter and Richard Sutcliffe proposed that an atlas publication should be produced to celebrate the twentieth anniversary of the branch in 2005. This book is the result.

Richard Sutcliffe (left), Pru Williams (centre) and Graham Irving (right) – previous chairmen and chairlady of the Glasgow branch

Chairmen of the Glasgow and South West Scotland branch of Butterfly Conservation

1985-1986	F. Gerald Rodway
1986-1987	Dr Michael Kibby
1987-1999	Richard Sutcliffe
1999-2000	Graham Irving
2000-2002	Mrs Prudence Williams
2002-2006	David Welham

Members of Butterfly Conservation who live in the branch area automatically become members of the branch. Members from elsewhere can join the branch on payment of the appropriate branch subscription. In 2005 there were approximately 200 branch members and 12,000 members of the National Society.

Large Heath, subspecies *scotica*, a butterfly that is vulnerable to habitat loss and which requires targeted monitoring. This photograph was taken by the late Gerry Rodway. Gerry was a passionate photographer of butterflies and shared his enthusiasm with members of the branch. One of his main aims was to try to improve the plight of the Large Heath in South West Scotland

Recording and Survey Methods

Butterfly records are essential to allow conservationists to assess the status of each species. Even within the ten-year period covered by this atlas, the status of several species has changed dramatically. Several species have declined – the Dingy Skipper in particular, while others have expanded their ranges rapidly – the Orange-tip, Peacock and Ringlet being notable, and two species appear to be established in South West Scotland for the first time in many years – the Holly Blue and Comma.

Early Recording

George Thomson's 1980 book, *The Butterflies of Scotland*, was the first book to give distribution maps of butterflies just in Scotland. The historical data was obtained from a wide number of sources, but was still fairly limited, as there were then few butterfly recorders in Scotland to provide records. However, it gave an incentive for recorders to note new localities. The *Atlas of Butterflies in Britain and Ireland* (Heath *et al.*, 1984), also stimulated recording, to 'fill the gaps'.

From 1985 up to 1994, branch recording was fairly basic. Records were entered manually onto summary sheets species by species, which was very time consuming. Producing distribution maps was almost impossible. The 10km records from the branch were however provided for use in *The Moths and Butterflies of Great Britain and Ireland Volume 7* (Emmet & Heath, 1990).

Recording is an important tool. In 1988 the Forestry Commission asked the branch to do a survey at Mabie Forest near Dumfries (see page 118). The results confirmed its importance as one of the best sites in Scotland and led to the establishment of a Forest Nature Reserve. Since then a butterfly transect

Butterfly transect walk at Cathkin Braes Country Park, Glasgow. Transect walks are an important monitoring tool of butterflies

has been set up and is walked by branch committee member Jessie MacKay as part of the national Butterfly Monitoring Scheme (see page 23).

At this stage the branch still collected records from the whole of Scotland. A Scottish Butterfly Report was produced in 1991 by Richard Sutcliffe, covering the years 1988-1990. This indicated earliest and latest sightings and location data. As there were very few members of Butterfly Conservation in Scotland at that time, the records were very limited.

Recording for the Atlas Project

The First Five Years (1995-1999)

In 1993 Jim Asher, Butterfly Conservation's national recorder, developed his *Levana* computer program for the processing of butterfly records. This program enabled branch recorders in most branches in Britain to enter records in the same format, and to produce distribution maps. This allowed the establishment of Butterfly Conservation's *Butterfly Net* – the first serious attempt by the Society to combine records from all the branches in a usable form. At the same time two new recording forms were produced – a site record form, for recording all sightings at a particular place, and a casual records form, for all other records. The *Levana* programme has subsequently been enhanced and improved allowing the data to be analysed in many different ways.

From 1995-1999 efforts concentrated on the Butterflies for the New Millennium project (BNM), with the aim of producing a Millennium Atlas covering the whole of Great Britain and Ireland.

HAVE YOU SEEN AN ORANGE TIP BUTTERFLY THIS YEAR?

Postcards like this were used to promote a detailed survey of Orange-tips in 1997 and 1998 to establish the extent of the spread of this species in Scotland. The photograph was taken by Gerry Rodway

To encourage more records for this initiative, and get more people recording, a series of surveys were organised by the branch. These concentrated on a few key species, that were regarded as rare, under-recorded or changing their distribution. One was for the Orange-tip. At that time the species was expanding quite dramatically in the Central Belt of Scotland and many people were seeing it for the first time. Initial surveys had been run through BRISC (Biological Recording in Scotland Campaign) in the 1980s. In 1997 a postcard survey was organised by Paul Kirkland. Hundreds of postcards with a male Orange-tip on one side, and a form for recording sightings on the other side, were sent out. Recorders sent their postcards to Richard Sutcliffe, who entered all the data into *Levana*. This was repeated again in 1998. A press release was issued and was taken up by large numbers of Scottish newspapers which resulted in some excellent publicity. As a result there were a staggering 750 records of Orange-tips sent in from all over Scotland. There were hundreds of sightings in areas where the butterfly had not been seen before.

In 1995 the Scottish Diurnal Lepidoptera Project (SDLP) was set up to investigate the status of what were believed to be Scotland's rarest and most endangered butterflies (Chequered Skipper, Dingy Skipper, Small Blue, Northern Brown Argus, Marsh Fritillary, Pearl-bordered Fritillary and Mountain Ringlet), plus several species of day-flying moths. The SDLP was co-ordinated by the Institute of Terrestrial Ecology (now the Centre for Ecology & Hydrology). As part of the project they also did a detailed survey of the Mountain Ringlet on Ben Lawers in Perthshire.

This was followed up by a Mountain Ringlet postcard survey in 1999, along the same lines of the Orange-tip survey – this time targeted at hillwalkers. It produced a reasonably good response, with new records coming in from several areas. Unfortunately a few records obviously referred to Scotch Argus and one person kindly confirmed that there were no Mountain Ringlets seen in Edinburgh!

From 1998 there was a UK-wide Pearl-bordered Fritillary survey, co-ordinated by Butterfly Conservation. This resulted in dozens of new records.

There were also specific surveys for Chequered Skipper and Marsh Fritillary.

In 1998 it became obvious that some parts of South West Scotland were generally under recorded – mainly remote areas. Several volunteers were given details of areas needing surveyed and these were visited during 1998 and 1999. This targeted recording helped to fill in most of the gaps, so that there was almost complete coverage of all 10km squares in our area over the five year survey period. However, this meant that in some cases a 10km square had only been visited once – and depending on the time of the visit, the recorder would inevitably miss some species which flew at a different time of the year. This shows up particularly in the case of Kintyre, which had only a few visits in 1995-1999, but which has been very well recorded since then.

The results of the first five years were published in the *Millennium Atlas of Butterflies in Britain and Ireland* (Asher *et al*. 2001).

Specific surveys were undertaken for some butterflies including the Marsh Fritillary to ensure coverage was as complete as possible. Mating pair, the female is left of the male and has a large, egg-laden abdomen.

The Second Five Years (2000-2004)

The recording effort throughout the branch area is very dependent on individual recorders. Coverage of some areas has been much better since 2000. In Mull, Kintyre and other parts of Argyll, where groups have got together to actively record their local areas, there are many more records. This has been partly as a direct result of numerous butterfly workshops run by Butterfly Conservation in 2003 and 2004.

Other areas are less well recorded, for example in Ayrshire, where Fraser Simpson and Bill Davidson used to record in nearly every 1km square, for the Ayrshire Bird Report, during the first five year period, but both moved away from the branch area during the second five year period.

The Orange-tip survey in 1997 and 1998 resulted in large numbers of records for this species. There have been fewer records for Orange-tips in the later period as the species was not specifically targeted. It is also noticeable that some recorders did not record common species. As a result, a few species may look less common than they really are, simply due to lack of records, rather than a true absence. The outbreak of foot and mouth disease in 2001 also resulted in many areas being inaccessible for butterfly recording.

Distribution Maps

The distribution maps in this atlas cover the years 1995-2004, these include 33,874 records for the 1995-1999 period and 22,570 records for 2000-2004. The data was originally entered in *Levana* and then transferred to *MapMate* for publication purposes.

All the data received had to be verified. All grid references were checked and records of butterflies that appeared to be outside their usual area or flight periods had to be confirmed.

There are two maps for each species. Each map shows records for a particular species produced at a 5km square (5km x 5km) resolution. This is a higher resolution than that of the 10km square used in the *Millennium Atlas* (Asher et al, 2001). Each dot on the map represents at least one record within that 5km square. One map shows the distribution of each species between the two five year periods of data, and the other map shows the abundance of records received for each species.

Distribution Map – showing the location of all records received for all species between 1995-2004 for each 5km square.

Abundance Map – showing the number of all records received for all species between 1995-2004 for each 5km square.

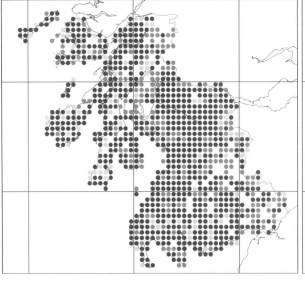 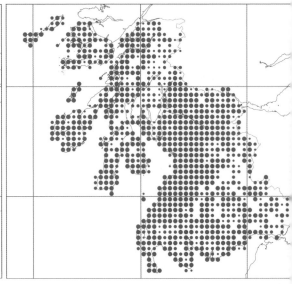

Key
- 1995-1999
- 2000-2004
- Both five year periods

Key
- 1 record
- 2-9 records
- 10+ records

Phenograms

The phenograms show the flight period recorded for each species during 1995-2004. The colours represent an indication of relative abundance, with low numbers shown by the cool colours blue and green, and a high number of records shown by the warm colours of yellow, orange and brown.

For example, the phenogram of the Ringlet below shows early emergent dates of mid-June, with an exceptional record in late May. Numbers build up to a peak in mid-July then fall to the beginning of August until only an occasional record was observed in late August.

Ringlet 1995-2004

| Jan | Feb | Mar | Apr | May | Jun | Jul | Aug | Sep | Oct | Nov | Dec |

The Butterfly Monitoring Scheme and Future Recording

Records from the Butterfly Monitoring Scheme co-ordinated by the Centre for Hydrology and Ecology and other independent transects have been very useful in establishing trends (see Brereton *et al.* 2006). Transects are fixed routes that are walked weekly between April and September, using a standardised method of recording the butterflies seen. In recent years many

Julie Stoneman (centre) leading a Butterfly Conservation Scotland workshop at Mabie Forest, near Dumfries to encourage the recording of butterflies

more independent transects have been set up in our area. These will hopefully continue to run, allowing the relative abundance of species to be monitored over a longer period.

Butterfly distributions are not static and it is important to continue recording butterflies in South West Scotland. We would welcome any butterfly records from anywhere in the area. Records will be used for nature conservation, research, education and public information, but remain the property of the individual recorders at all times.

Recording sheets are available through Butterfly Conservation (see Useful Contacts, page 152).

The minimum data required is grid reference, locality name, date, species seen and the recorder's name. Ideally information on numbers of adults seen, plus any eggs, larvae, pupae, habitat information and any behavioural observations should also be provided.

South West Scotland

(opposite) A female Chequered Skipper on Bugle, a favoured nectar source.

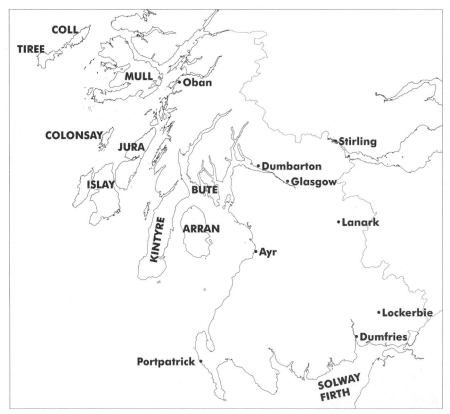

The Current Status of Butterflies in South West Scotland

During the ten year recording period (1995-2004) there were 32 species of butterfly observed on a regular basis in South West Scotland. A further three butterfly species were recorded as occasional visitors. This represents approximately half of the total of butterfly species recorded in Britain as a whole.

The restricted number of species occurring in South West Scotland is mainly due to an unfavourable climate, being wetter and cooler than the south of England. Another factor is the underlying geology and associated soils, which do not support many of the caterpillar foodplants that are required by several species of butterfly found in southern England, such as those that are dependent on limestone.

But here populations of Chequered Skipper, Northern Brown Argus, Marsh Fritillary, Pearl-bordered Fritillary, Mountain Ringlet, Scotch Argus and Large Heath are British strongholds.

The following section describes each species in detail. Occasional personal observations noted in the text are abbreviated as (pers.obs.) and personal communication as (pers.com.).

A close up of the antennae of the Chequered Skipper. The female (right) has more black to the club base than the male (left)

Identification

A brightly marked skipper with a pattern of golden yellow against a dark brown background on the upperwings, and a paler, intricate chequered pattern on the underwings. The sexes are similar although the female is usually larger and paler and more recognisable when the abdomen is swollen with eggs. There is also a tendency for the underneath of the antennae tips to be different with males having more yellow and females more black, as shown above. The head and thorax are large and broad in comparison to the body, and the wings appear under-sized. Despite the relatively small size of the wings the butterflies can disappear from view quickly with a rapid burst of flight.

Life Cycle

Adults emerge in mid-May and are conspicuous as they nectar on Bugle, Tormentil, Marsh Thistle, Bluebell, White Clover and other available flowers. The butterflies are short lived and by the end of June the flight period is over. In contrast the caterpillars are long lived. They hatch from white eggs laid singly on Purple Moor-grass from early June and feed on grass blades until late October or early November. They then over-winter in silk-wrapped grass blades, emerge in early April and pupate in late April. An excellent summary of the life cycle and behaviour is detailed in the Butterfly Conservation publication, *The Chequered Skipper* (1996) by Neil Ravenscroft.

Chequered Skipper
DISTRIBUTION

Chequered Skipper
ABUNDANCE

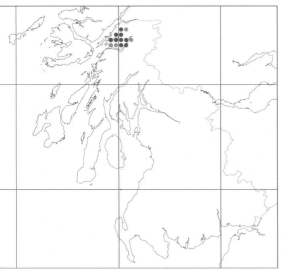

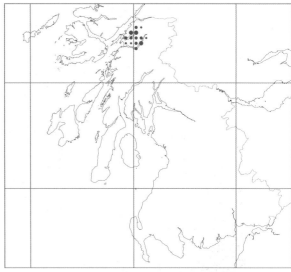

Chequered Skipper 1995-2004											
Jan	Feb	Mar	Apr	May	Jun	Jul	Aug	Sep	Oct	Nov	Dec

Habitat and Distribution

The Chequered Skipper is very localised in Scotland and is found in the north west corner of our branch area in Argyll. It is found on the lower glen slopes along the shores of Loch Etive and Loch Creran and further north into the Highland region as far as Loch Arkaig, where Butterfly Conservation has a nature reserve at Allt Mhuic (NN121912). The favoured habitat is open grassland that has mineral enrichment from flushing and is surrounded by woodland, usually Oak, Birch and Alder that creates wind shelter and provides local warm spots. The habitat often contains Bog Myrtle, an indicator of mineral flushing and may be beneficial in creating shelter for the developing caterpillar.

The distribution of the Chequered Skipper is not limited by habitat as suitable habitat occurs in other parts of South West Scotland especially southern Argyll, Dunbartonshire, and parts of Stirlingshire and Dumfries & Galloway. The distribution in Argyll is probably limited by climate with relatively mild winter conditions occurring with warm, wet summers that provide the ideal conditions to sustain lush growth of the Purple Moor-grass. Recent reports of the species on Mull still require confirmation.

Status

The Chequered Skipper appears to have a relatively stable population at present. As a consequence of the limited area that the Chequered Skipper occupies in Scotland, numbers and distribution will always need to be monitored and habitats managed to maintain pockets of open grassland in wooded areas. If the maintenance of woodland glades and way leaves beneath power lines continue, together with the restriction of sheep grazing in habitats occupied by the Chequered Skipper, then the population should continue to be stable. If the current trend of mild winters and climate warming continues it is possible that the Chequered Skipper might increase its range.

Male Large Skipper

Identification

The Large Skipper is currently the only 'orange' skipper found in Scotland although the Small Skipper is pushing northwards in its range in England and is close to the Scottish border. The Large Skipper is a robust butterfly. The males can easily be told apart from females by the presence of a black line (sex-brand) on each forewing. The females are slightly larger than males and also have more contrasting yellow-orange dappled markings on the upper forewings and underwings.

At rest, when basking in the sun the forewings are not held flat but angled in readiness for flight. When active both sexes readily nectar from flowers and the males seek out females amongst grass clumps or chase away rival males that enter a territory. Flight is busy and rapid, appearing as an orange blur.

Life Cycle

The Large Skipper spends most of its life as a caterpillar and adults have a short flight time in South West Scotland, being on the wing during June and July. The female lays whitish eggs singly on grasses, particularly Cock's-foot and occasionally Purple Moor-grass. The dark bluish-green caterpillar constructs a grass tube using silk threads attached to each edge of the leaf blade. This forms a shelter from which the caterpillar emerges to feed on the leaf during the summer and autumn. It is slow-growing and mainly a nocturnal feeder. The caterpillar hibernates in the grass tube during the winter and forms a chrysalis the following May in a nest of grass blades held together with silk.

DISTRIBUTION   ABUNDANCE

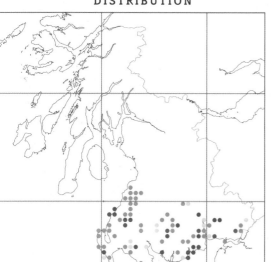

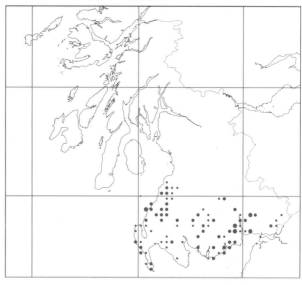

Large Skipper 1995-2004

| Jan | Feb | Mar | Apr | May | Jun | Jul | Aug | Sep | Oct | Nov | Dec |

Female Large Skipper

Distribution

In South West Scotland the Large Skipper is confined to Dumfries & Galloway and South Ayrshire, but it is widespread in this area. Sites such as Portpatrick, Feoch Meadow, Rockcliffe and Mabie Forest are good places to see the butterfly.

It is most commonly seen at flower-rich grassland habitats along the coastal fringe but also favours woodland edges and open glades. It may also venture into gardens, particularly if there is a wide variety of flowers to feed on. At the coastal sites it can be seen flying alongside the Northern Brown Argus as it drinks nectar from Bloody Cranesbill and Thyme.

Status

Currently the population appears to be stable in numbers and it is not of conservation concern. The Large Skipper is one of the butterflies that would be predicted to expand its range northwards as the climate becomes generally warmer.

The Dingy Skipper, a species in decline in South West Scotland

Identification

Named for its brown coloration, the Dingy Skipper may not be the most attractive of butterflies but it does have plenty of charm and character. Both sexes are similar in colour, having a uniform pale brown background flecked with white. The butterflies are short lived and after a few days from emergence the wings start to get worn and they soon become damaged at the edges.

Life Cycle

The green-orange eggs are laid singly on the leaves or leaf stalks of Birdsfoot-trefoil or Greater Birdsfoot-trefoil in June. The caterpillar is slow to develop and feeds throughout the year before hibernating during winter in a tent of leaves spun together with silk threads. It pupates in the nest of leaves in April and then emerges as an adult butterfly in May and June.

Typical behaviour of the adult is to spend lots of time basking in the sun on bare ground with its wings held wide open. Males hold temporary territories. They interrupt their sun bathing with rapid bouts of buzzing flight to intercept and chase away a passing male and then return near to where it first settled, or to court a passing female. Some spiral flights between combatant males can be lengthy affairs and last for several minutes.

Dingy Skipper

DISTRIBUTION

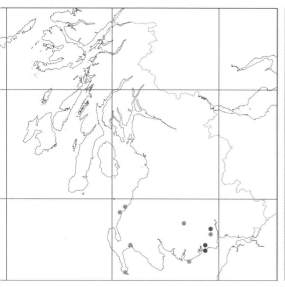

Dingy Skipper

ABUNDANCE

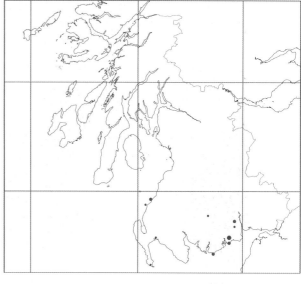

Dingy Skipper 1995-2004

Jan	Feb	Mar	Apr	May	Jun	Jul	Aug	Sep	Oct	Nov	Dec

Habitat and Distribution

In South West Scotland the Dingy Skipper currently appears to be confined to Dumfries & Galloway with no recent records from South Ayrshire, although it may have been overlooked at some sites.

The butterflies are most frequently seen along the coast, often near a path where there is plenty of bare sand or gravely ground adjacent to the larval food plant.

The results of our survey indicate it is a butterfly that is rapidly declining. Despite concerted efforts to look for the Dingy Skipper during 2000 to 2004 a core population could only be found near Dalbeattie. In 2005 a population was rediscovered at Garheugh Rocks, Luce Bay (NX265504, J. Black pers.obs.) to give some hope that further colonies will be found.

Status

Sadly the Dingy Skipper is in rapid decline and it is the rarest of the 32 species of butterfly found regularly in South West Scotland.

The reason for the decline is unclear as there is plenty of suitable habitat and the larval food plant is common. It is possible that changes in land use and habitat succession may be a factor in its decline as it prefers land that has a patchwork of bare soil resulting from frequent erosion. The decline is echoed in other parts of Britain and Europe and it is clearly a species requiring assistance if it is to be prevented from becoming extinct in our branch area.

Identification

This migrant from North Africa and Southern Europe is the only orange-yellow butterfly likely to be seen in South West Scotland. It could be confused with the Brimstone, but this is a very rare visitor, or with bright yellow forms of the Small White and Green-veined White, which are also very rare. These three species can be easily separated from the Clouded Yellow when seen at close range.

The upper wing surfaces of the Clouded Yellow are normally only seen when the butterfly is in flight. The male has a broad solid black margin to the orange-yellow wings whereas the female has the black band interrupted with several yellow spots. Some females are of the form *helice* and have the upperwings a pale yellow or white. They are very noticeable in flight and the form is not uncommon.

When at rest or feeding from flowers the wings are always closed. Both sexes have similar underside markings. The wing margin is edged with pink and the hindwing has a distinctive, central white figure of 8 marking, although the upper white circle may be very small or absent. A series of pink or black dots is located near the wing edge, although in some individuals these may be absent or much reduced. A conspicuous black dot on the underside of the forewing is always present.

The eyes of both sexes are a beautiful emerald green which contrast with the pink colouration of the antennae and upper head.

Life Cycle

In most years when immigrants arrive they are generally first seen in May or June and breed here. There will then be a larger second brood later in the summer. In 1992 there was even a partial third brood, with some adults being seen well into October. The pearl-white egg is laid singly on clovers and other legumes. The green caterpillar develops quickly and is fully mature in about four weeks. The green chrysalis is formed on a plant stem near the ground. The butterfly emerges after about three weeks. It is unable to survive the winter in South West Scotland.

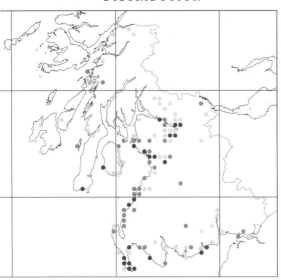

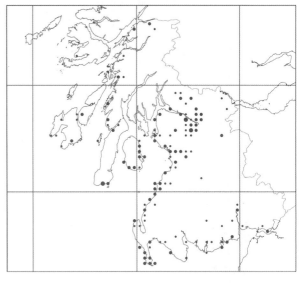

Clouded Yellow 1995-2004

| Jan | Feb | Mar | Apr | May | Jun | Jul | Aug | Sep | Oct | Nov | Dec |

Habitat and Distribution

The most common route of most of the migratory butterflies into South West Scotland is along the coasts of the Irish Sea. The Clouded Yellow is no exception and appears to particularly hug the coastline as most records are from coastal sightings.

The Clouded Yellow is a strong flyer and will quickly pass through an area, occasionally stopping to nectar on clovers, thistles, Lesser Knapweed, Ragwort and other composites. The butterfly does venture inland and flower-rich meadows, large gardens and urban waste ground are favoured habitats. A large number of Clouded Yellows were seen in the City of Glasgow in 1992, nectaring on flowers at sites of urban waste ground.

Status

An unpredictable migrant that is unable to survive our winter. Occasional invasions result in large numbers of butterflies being recorded. The major invasion of 1992 led to hundreds of sightings between late April and late October (Sutcliffe, 1994). This was because the butterflies, when leaving France and Spain, were blown out over the Atlantic and came from the west, directly into Northern Ireland and western Scotland, rather than moving north through England.

Further minor invasions occurred in 1998 and again in 2000 with butterflies seen from mid-June to late September. During the survey period (1995-2004) there has been a marked increase in the number of records received when compared to historical records (Thomson, 1980). The Clouded Yellow is now recorded on an annual basis in South West Scotland.

Female Large White on Tufted Vetch

Identification

The Large White is often referred to as the Cabbage White as the female will lay a cluster of eggs on cultivated cabbages and other brassicas. The caterpillars will then strip the plant to its leaf stalks. Although gardeners may take a dislike to it, the Large White is nonetheless a very attractive butterfly and its large size makes it an impressive sight when flying. The female has two black spots on the upper forewing, whereas the male is white on the upper forewing, without spots. The female also has a pale yellow wash on the upper hindwings, whereas this is white in the male. Both sexes have black spots on the underside of the forewing. The wing tips are black and more heavily marked than those of the Small White.

Life Cycle

The adult butterfly can be seen from May to September. In addition to the female laying eggs, as a cluster, on cultivated brassicas, the yellow-orange eggs may also be laid on Garden Nasturtium. Wild crucifers may also be eaten and at coastal sites the Sea Radish may occasionally be used. The green and yellow, black speckled caterpillars have a conspicuous yellow dorsal stripe. They live in loose groups and give off a pungent smell to deter predators. This same smell may attract parasitic *Cotesisa glomerata* wasps which lay eggs within the caterpillar. The parasitized caterpillar will be killed when the mature wasp grubs emerge from their host. The over-wintering stage is as a chrysalis, which is often formed on walls, outbuildings and on roofs inside a shed or garage.

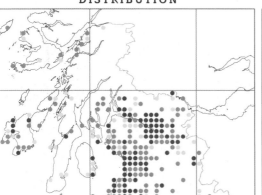

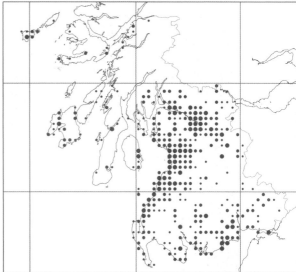

Large White 1995-2004

Jan	Feb	Mar	Apr	May	Jun	Jul	Aug	Sep	Oct	Nov	Dec

Caterpillars feeding on Sea Radish
(Ardmore Point, Dunbartonshire)

Habitat and Distribution

In South West Scotland the Large White is not as common as it is in southern England. Indeed the resident population may be small, for in some years the Large White is uncommon. In other years greater numbers are seen, particularly in August and September, as a result of a migratory influx from other parts of Britain and Europe.

The Large White is patchily distributed in South West Scotland being most commonly observed in parks and gardens and along the coastal fringe. It is a highly mobile species and will move from garden to garden feeding on the nectar of flowers such as Buddleia, Lavender and Verbena. In the wider countryside flower-rich meadows are favoured with Lesser Knapweed, Spear Thistle and Creeping Thistle frequently visited as nectar sources.

Status

The Large White is currently not a species of conservation concern and the numbers seen each year in South West Scotland partly depend on the migration of individuals from Europe.

Small White *Pieris rapae*

Small White on Garlic Mustard

Upperwings of a female

Identification

The Small White is very difficult to distinguish from the Green-veined White when in flight and close inspection is required to tell them apart, particularly as they often share the same habitat. When seen close up they are easily separated from the Green-veined White as they lack the dark markings on the veins. They can also be difficult to distinguish from small individuals of the Large White when in flight. Both sexes are similar in appearance although the female has more defined black spots on both upper and lower wings. The female has two black dots on the upper forewing whereas the male has only one black dot.

Life Cycle

It is one of the earliest butterflies to emerge in Spring and it may be seen in a garden during a sunny April day. It is double brooded and is on the wing from April to September. The second brood is usually more numerous and some females can have a very yellow look.

The pale yellow eggs are laid singly. In gardens the caterpillar will feed on a variety of crucifers including the cultivated Cabbage and Garden Nasturtium, and at coastal sites the Sea Radish may be used. The pale green, velvety caterpillars grow quickly and mature in about three weeks. The second brood caterpillar forms a chrysalis which over-winters. The chrysalis is formed on trees, fences, walls or buildings.

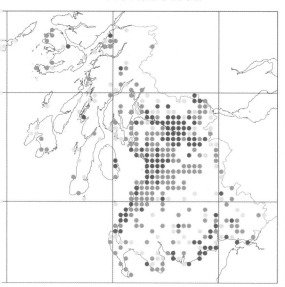

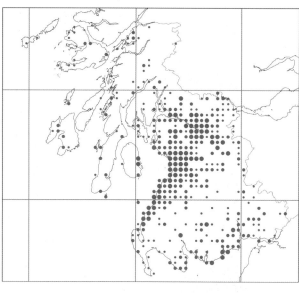

Small White 1995-2004

| Jan | Feb | Mar | Apr | May | Jun | Jul | Aug | Sep | Oct | Nov | Dec |

Habitat and Distribution

In South West Scotland the Small White has a widespread distribution but it is much less common than the Green-veined White.

It is most commonly found in parks, gardens and coastal areas and favours drier habitats compared with the Green-veined White. The Small White appears to be most numerous in urban areas and near habitation possibly as a result of an increase in caterpillar foodplants such as cultivated brassicas.

Usually found singly or in small numbers the Small White is highly mobile as it seeks a mate, searches for a suitable egg-laying site or a flower to feed on nectar.

Status

The Small White currently has a stable distribution and population size and it is not a species of conservation concern in South West Scotland.

Mating pair, the female is below the male

Identification

At a distance the Green-veined White is almost impossible to tell apart from a Small White or a smaller sized Large White. But at close inspection it has greenish-black venation, particularly on the underside of the hindwings. The white tips of the antennae are a further conspicuous feature. The sexes are similar to each other but the female generally has more pronounced markings. The amount of vein colour-ation is variable. The second brood females can be more yellow and closely resemble a Small White.

Life Cycle

The butterfly is on the wing from late April to early October with peaks in May and August which reflect that it is double brooded. At some sites, such as flower-rich wet meadows, there are distinct colonies and males can be seen flying back and forth in their search for females. The Green-veined White can also be a highly mobile species and can cover large distances in search of flowers for nectar or in the case of males the constant search for females.

The pale yellow eggs are laid singly on the leaves of a variety of crucifers such as Cuckoo Flower and Garlic Mustard. The egg-laying female flies just above the ground seeking food plants that are in damp sheltered places. The pale green caterpillar grows quickly in the summer and is mature in about four weeks. The caterpillar from the second brood forms a chrysalis in September and is the over-wintering stage. The caterpillar is similar to that of the Small White but lacks a pale dorsal stripe and has only one yellow spot around the spiracles whereas the Small White has a pale dorsal line and has two yellow spots at the side of each body segment.

DISTRIBUTION

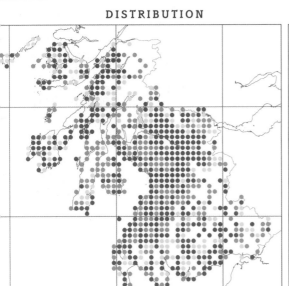

ABUNDANCE

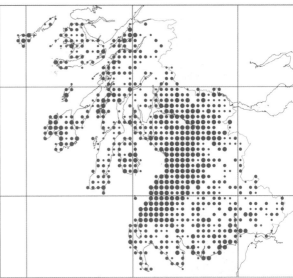

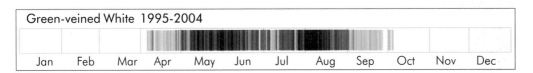

Green-veined White 1995-2004

| Jan | Feb | Mar | Apr | May | Jun | Jul | Aug | Sep | Oct | Nov | Dec |

Habitat and Distribution

The Green-veined White is probably the most common butterfly in South West Scotland. It has a widespread distribution and can be locally abundant. Indeed it may often be the only butterfly encountered on wet, rush dominated flushes on hill slopes.

It favours wet grassland habitats but can also be found in other habitats including gardens, woodland edges and moorland.

The Green-veined white may also congregate on open ground, along a track near a shallow puddle, or the site of water run off, to drink dissolved salts and minerals.

The Green-veined White far outnumbers the Small White and Large White to the extent that in many parts of South West Scotland almost all white butterflies encountered in mid-summer will be Green-veined Whites.

Male Green-veined White

Status

The Green-veined White is one of the few butterflies in South West Scotland that can be classified as common. The generally wetter climate compared to other parts of Britain means that the favoured habitat of wet grassland with rushes is widespread and able to support and maintain a healthy population of this attractive butterfly.

Identification

The Orange-tip is one of our most distinctive butterflies. The male is unmistakable, being a medium sized white butterfly with orange and black wingtips. The female is less conspicuous, lacking the orange markings and at a distance it can be mistaken for a Small White or Green-veined White. When seen closely, the female can be identified by the single black spot near the front edge of the forewing, and the faint pattern of the underwing showing through from below. In both sexes the tips of the forewings are more rounded than the other whites and the underside of the hindwings have a mottled, moss green pattern.

Life Cycle

The butterfly is on the wing from mid April until mid-June, but it is sometimes seen as late as mid-July and even into August. In 1988 a male was seen in September at Lochwinnoch and M. Dowsland found a male at Canderside, Stonehouse on 24th September 1994, suggesting a second brood in some years.

The males generally emerge about a week earlier than the females and patrol up and down suitable patches of habitat in search of females. The female lays the bottle-shaped egg singly beneath the flowerbud. It is white at first, but turns bright orange after a day or two. The emerging caterpillar is pale orange with black hairs when young, but as it matures it becomes blue-green on top and dark green underneath. The caterpillar feeds on the seed pods and lies along the top of a seed pod of its foodplant when resting. Although beautifully camouflaged, it is fairly easy to find in June and July. The most common foodplants are Cuckoo Flower and Garlic Mustard, although Dame's Violet, Honesty and other crucifers may be selected. The caterpillar generally pupates in dense vegetation, usually close to shrubs. The chrysalis is very difficult to find and resembles a thorn on a stem. It is either pale brown or green and is the over-wintering stage. On occasion the chrysalis can stay dormant for two winters (Futter, K. pers.obs. at Dumbarton – see also Emmet & Heath, 1990).

Orange-tip

DISTRIBUTION

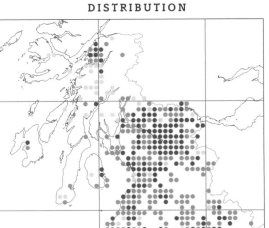

Orange-tip

ABUNDANCE

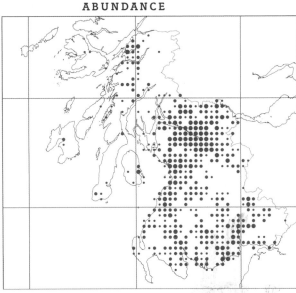

Orange-tip 1995-2004											
Jan	Feb	Mar	Apr	May	Jun	Jul	Aug	Sep	Oct	Nov	Dec

Habitat and Distribution

Up until the early 1980s, the Orange-tip had a restricted distribution in South West Scotland to parts of Dumfries & Galloway, and a few colonies in South Ayrshire and Lanarkshire. In the mid 1980s the species started to spread (Futter & Futter 1998, Sutcliffe & Kirkland 1998). The expansion was rapid and it is now found throughout South West Scotland. The increase in range of the Orange-tip was assisted by a similar expansion in range of Garlic Mustard in some parts of South West Scotland (K. Futter pers.obs., see also BSBI Atlas data – Perring & Walters 1990; Preston et al. 2002).

Orange-tips are most likely to be found close to where their caterpillar foodplants occur. The Orange-tip favours two general types of habitat, either drier sites along a hedgerow or woodland edge, where Garlic Mustard is the favoured foodplant, or at wetter sites of marshy grassland with adjacent scrub, where Cuckoo Flower is the favoured foodplant. It is also quite happy in a garden setting providing the

caterpillar foodplant is present. The largest number of butterflies will be found in habitats where the caterpillar foodplant is abundant. This is important because as the caterpillar feeds on seed pods, an individual caterpillar may require several plants to survive, particularly if feeding on Cuckoo Flower. If two caterpillars are in competition for a limited supply of seed pods they can become cannibalistic. This situation is much less frequent on Garlic Mustard due to the much larger size of the seed pods and the plant in general. Indeed several caterpillars can be found on a single, large plant of Garlic Mustard.

Status

The Orange-tip is now widespread in South West Scotland, and appears to be commoner now than at any time in the past and is not a species of conservation concern. It is likely that this spread is as a direct result of climate change, which also may have resulted in earlier emergence dates in April.

The Green Hairstreak may roost among Birch leaves

Identification

When the sun highlights the emerald green wings of the Green Hairstreak it reveals one of our most beautiful butterflies. Both sexes of this small butterfly are similar in appearance. When perched on vegetation they never open their wings but tilt the green undersides towards the sun, to gain maximum warmth.

The colour of green can be quite variable. Typically, both the undersides of the forewing and hindwing are varying shades of brilliant green. Some individuals have a turquoise-green lower underwing that shades to brown at the wing edge and the underside of the forewing has more brown than green. Variability in appearance includes the presence or absence of white dots on both the upper and lower underwings and some individuals have a bronze leading edge to the forewings. When the Green Hairstreak roosts among Birch leaves on heathland sites they are well camouflaged as the white flecking matches the leaf edge and the brown-bronze wing edges are similar to buds. They are also well camouflaged resting on Blaeberry leaves and Heather.

Life Cycle

The Green Hairstreak is a short-lived butterfly living about two weeks and emergence is from late April to late June, with a peak in numbers during mid May. The eggs are pale green and both the egg and the green caterpillar are difficult to find on the food plant. Although Blaeberry is the most common food plant at wet heathland and bog sites, the Cross-leaved Heath may also be used. At drier sites such as along the coastal fringe both Birdsfoot-trefoil and Gorse may be the foodplant. The chrysalis is formed just below the surface of the ground and there may be an association with ants.

The males are territorial and will intercept any passing male, resulting in a short spiral flight until one departs. Their

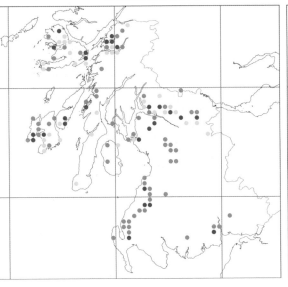

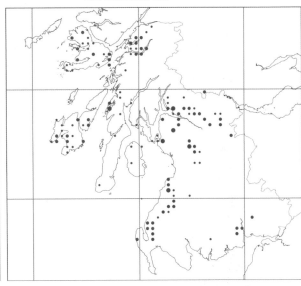

Green Hairstreak 1995-2004											
Jan	Feb	Mar	Apr	May	Jun	Jul	Aug	Sep	Oct	Nov	Dec

flight is very quick and busy and they can be difficult to follow. When flying they appear black or dark brown rather than green as a result of the dark upper wing surfaces. The upper wings are rarely revealed but can on occasion be seen when the wings are rubbed against each other in a circular motion, to release pheromones and scent scales.

Habitat and Distribution

The habitat preference in South West Scotland is wet heathland with occasional Birch which provides wind shelter and a locally warm microclimate. Some very wet blanket bog sites are also occupied which do not have Birch, but these usually have some form of shelter from the wind in the form of an adjacent woodland or topographical wind break. On exposed heathland, colonies can be found in stream-cut gullies which provide the all important shelter from the wind.

The Green Hairstreak can also be found on marshy grassland, flying alongside the Marsh Fritillary, and in open woodland in the company of Chequered Skipper and Small Copper.

Many records of the Green Hairstreak are of single individuals or a small colony. Larger heathland sites can accommodate greater numbers where it is possible to see 50-100 individuals on a visit. At Flanders Moss NNR several thousand individuals have been recorded on a single visit (M. Usher pers.com.).

Status

The Green Hairstreak in South West Scotland has a patchy distribution, constrained by suitable habitat. Small colonies can be easily overlooked and may be under recorded. Although some sites contain good numbers, the Green Hairstreak cannot be regarded as a common butterfly and colonies need careful monitoring. Some colonies appear to have been lost in Dumfries & Galloway in recent years. Threats are from the drainage of wet heathland which results in a dense canopy of Birch, and from over-grazing of heathland by sheep which reduces food plant availability. Urban development and golf course develop-ment that fringes heathland are also threats.

Purple Hairstreak *Neozephyrus quercus*

The Purple Hairstreak is a canopy species and can be difficult to find when resting on an Oak leaf

Identification

The male Purple Hairstreak has a brilliant, dark purple sheen to the upperwings. The female has the purple colouring restricted to patches on the forewing on a black-brown background, but it is no less attractive. The upper hindwings of the female are a dark brown. The undersides of both sexes are similar, being silver-grey, broken by a ragged white line. A bright orange, black centred eye spot occurs at the lower wing edge of both sexes and they both have short tail wing extensions. The Purple Hairstreak typically rests with its wings closed but frequently opens them fully to bask in the sun.

Life Cycle

The life of the Purple Hairstreak is centred around the Oak, with a possible preference shown toward the Pedunculate Oak (*Quercus robur*) (K. Futter pers.obs.). The butterflies spend most of their lives in the canopy of Oak and adjacent Ash and Sycamore trees where they feed on aphid honeydew deposits on the leaf surface. The Purple Hairstreak is single brooded flying from mid-July to early September. During sunny weather they actively fly about the outer branches and occasionally descend to lower branches, sometimes venturing further away to bask in the sun on bracken fronds and other low herbage. The female is usually seen more than the males as she seeks out suitable egg laying sites. The white disc-shaped eggs are laid singly beside a bud on a branch that receives the full sun. The egg is the over-wintering stage and the caterpillar hatches in early April to feed on the developing leaves within the bud. The brown caterpillar is well camouflaged and resembles an Oak bud. The chrysalis is formed on the ground in early June. It attracts ants and may receive protecton in an ants' nest.

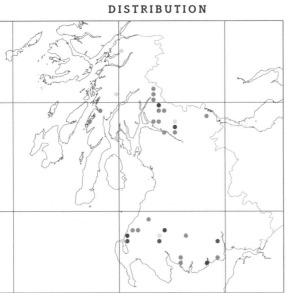

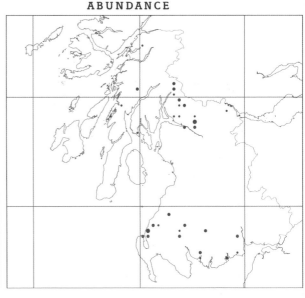

Purple Hairstreak 1995-2004

Jan	Feb	Mar	Apr	May	Jun	Jul	Aug	Sep	Oct	Nov	Dec

Habitat and Distribution

The Purple Hairstreak is almost certainly more widely distributed than records suggest. For example a strong colony was recorded at Coille Mor (NR408966) on Colonsay, 19th July 1977 (J. MacKay pers.obs.), but no records were received during the survey period.

The Purple Hairstreak is easily overlooked, as it usually flies high up in the canopy of Oak trees. It also tends to be more active in late afternoon and early evening. Both these factors may help to explain its apparent patchy distribution in South West Scotland. It does appear to be absent from many Oak woodlands, particularly those that are on acid soils, such as the woodlands along the Clyde and Avon river valleys in South Lanarkshire and does not seem to have been recorded where Sessile Oak (*Quercus petraea*) is dominant.

Stronghold populations are centred around Loch Lomond, especially the woods on the east side of the Loch in Stirlingshire, and in many of the Oak woodlands from Drymen to Mugdock Country Park and Garscadden Wood in Glasgow. Important colonies are also found in Argyll, Ayrshire and Dumfries & Galloway. Local colonies are also found in Renfrewshire, including a new observation in 2005 at Finlaystone. Many of the Purple Hairstreak colonies are located at Oak woodland where the ground flora is sparse, often with just a few grasses or occasional fern and this habitat type may be a limiting factor on the distribution. The chrysalis is known to attract ants and may be taken to their nest where it receives protection (see Thomas & Lewington 1991). This may also be a factor affecting distribution.

Status

The Purple Hairstreak is a widely distributed, but uncommon butterfly in South West Scotland although some Loch Lomondside colonies are large and appear stable. Further research is required to understand the habitat requirements of this beautiful butterfly in South West Scotland.

A female Small Copper on the flower of Bloody Cranesbill

Identification

The Small Copper is one of our smallest butterflies and also one of the most beautiful. The female is slightly larger than the male, but both are similarly marked having bright orange upper forewings with black dots. The upper hindwings are dark brown, often with small blue dots near the orange outer edge in the form *caeruleopunctata,* which appears to be more commonly shown by females. Variation includes a pale orange form and males that have the upper forewings with a beautiful green-purple sheen near the wing base. The underside of the hindwing is a pale brown. The copper colour is retained on the underside of the forewing which has the black dots faintly encircled with yellow.

Life Cycle

The male is highly territorial and very active. It will chase away any passing butterfly to return to a favoured perch, usually a horizontal grass blade or flower head. If a female passes by he will follow and settle close to her, or in front of her with wings rapidly vibrating to mark the onset of courtship.

The Small Copper is a short-lived butterfly but there are several generations in a year and it can be seen throughout the summer with a peak in numbers during August. The whitish eggs are laid on Common Sorrel, Sheep's Sorrel and occasionally on other Docks (*Rumex* spp.). The last generation caterpillar hibernates during the winter months. The chrysalis is formed among vegetation on the ground, where it is very well camouflaged.

DISTRIBUTION

ABUNDANCE

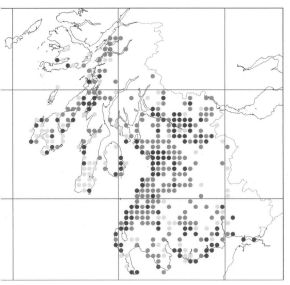

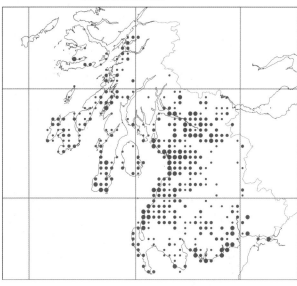

Small Copper 1995-2004											
Jan	Feb	Mar	Apr	May	Jun	Jul	Aug	Sep	Oct	Nov	Dec

Habitat and Distribution

In South West Scotland the Small Copper is widely distributed but it is a butterfly more often seen in warm summers, for in cooler years it can be scarce.

It is most commonly encountered where there are patches of open bare ground that get the full warmth of the sun. It is frequent at sandy, coastal habitats, often being encountered adjacent to the beach. At urban locations it can be found on sunny waste ground, on the verges beside paths and cycle-ways, and in flower-rich gardens.

The Small Copper seems very partial to feeding on small flowered composites, particularly Ragwort. The planting of daisies such as *Felicia* spp. and *Erigeron* spp. may attract the Small Copper to a garden.

Status

Although some years are poor the Small Copper can soon recover in numbers during a warm year. Currently the Small Copper has a stable population in South West Scotland and it is not a species of conservation concern.

Northern Brown Argus, *pallidior* form

Identification

The Northern Brown Argus is an attractive, diminutive butterfly. The Scottish subspecies *artaxerxes* has a white spot at the centre of each of the upper forewings. The name Argus refers to a Greek mythical beast with a hundred eyes, which relates to the eye spots on the underwings. The underside spots of the Northern Brown Argus are predominantly white with the occasional black dot.

In South West Scotland there are two colour forms of the Northern Brown Argus. The most common form has orange lunules at the edge of all upperwings of both males and females (see front cover) but there is also the form *pallidior* (above) which has pale yellow lunules. The background of the upperwings is either a grey-brown or a dark slate-brown – often looking almost metallic when fresh – which is attractively set against a white outer fringe along the wing edges. Both sexes are similar in appearance, although females have a greater number of orange or yellow lunules on the upper forewing.

Life Cycle

Individuals have been recorded from late May, but the butterfly is typically on the wing as a single brood from mid-June until the end of July, rarely lingering to August. In some years a second brood may be produced as fresh individuals have been seen in August (e.g. two freshly emerged individuals were seen at Balcreuchan Port, Bennane Head NX 099876 on 6th August 1992, J. Black pers.obs.). The males establish small territories to await a passing female. The territories are actively defended and an intruding male is confronted. A spiral flight follows to determine the victor. The white eggs are laid singly on the upper leaf surface of Common Rock-rose, which is thought to be the sole food plant. The small green caterpillar is long lived. It actively feeds during mid-summer until October when it over-winters in leaf litter. In April it resumes feeding until fully grown by mid-May when it pupates on the ground, among leaves.

DISTRIBUTION

ABUNDANCE

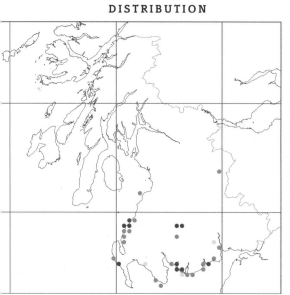

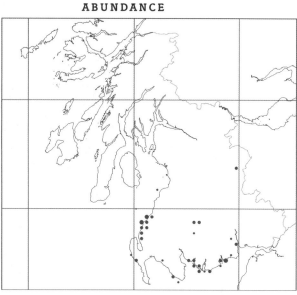

Northern Brown Argus 1995-2004											
Jan	Feb	Mar	Apr	May	Jun	Jul	Aug	Sep	Oct	Nov	Dec

Habitat and Distribution

The Northern Brown Argus is predominantly a coastal species found in South Ayrshire and Dumfries & Galloway, with the occasional inland site. There is a single locality in Lanarkshire, which is at the western limit of a wide distribution in the Pentland and Lammermuir Hills to the east. A few new sites have turned up following specific searches in Dumfries & Galloway and there may still be more colonies to be found elsewhere.

Its distribution in South West Scotland will always be restricted due to the limitations of geology – outcrops of limestone or base-rich rock that support Common Rock-rose. Favoured habitats are south facing slopes, sheltered from the wind, that have base-rich rocks. These typically accommodate a rich flora, usually indicated by Bloody Cranesbill, Thyme and Common Rock-rose.

Status

Generally the population of Northern Brown Argus is relatively stable in South West Scotland but it is small due to the restrictions of foodplant distribution. More research is required to evaluate if Common Rock-rose is the sole foodplant used in the wild. It is possible that Bloody Cranesbill and other Geraniums may be alternative foodplants (see Thomson, 1980). At Rockcliffe (see page 118) the Common Rock-rose is very local and the Northern Brown Argus has on occasion been most common at large patches of Bloody Cranesbill and Dove's-foot Cranesbill (K. Futter pers.obs.).

Some occupied sites are on steep slopes and erosion may threaten some local colonies. Some well known sites, such as those north of Lendalfoot, Ayrshire, have suffered from visitor pressure which has resulted in the erosion of parts of the habitat, particularly on steep slopes.

A male Common Blue basking in sunshine,
head down on a grass blade

Identification

A blue butterfly encountered in South West Scotland will almost certainly be a Common Blue. The only exception would be a Holly Blue, which is confined to a very few locations in Dumfries & Galloway. The male Common Blue has upperwings that vary from an intense bright blue to a less attractive blue-brown. The bright blue males are often larger in size and very conspicuous when flying in full sun. The female upperwings are brown and blue with orange margins. They typically have a higher proportion of blue coloration than those found in England and Wales and completely brown females are rare. The underwings of both sexes have many black spots encircled with white, and have orange markings near the outer edge.

Life Cycle

In South West Scotland the Common Blue is generally single brooded flying from June to September. In more northern locations there may be only a mid summer emergence from late July to early September. The whitish eggs are typically laid on Birdsfoot-trefoil or Greater Birdsfoot-trefoil, but White Clover and other low growing legumes may on occasion be selected. The green, grub-like caterpillar over-winters before pupating in the spring.

DISTRIBUTION   ABUNDANCE

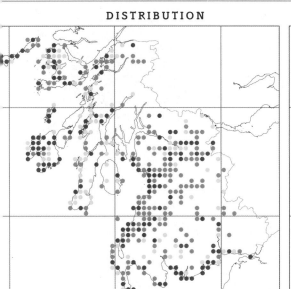
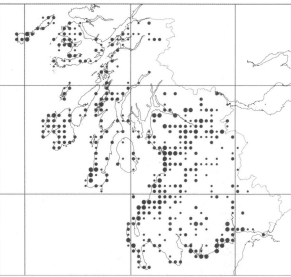

Common Blue 1995-2004

| Jan | Feb | Mar | Apr | May | Jun | Jul | Aug | Sep | Oct | Nov | Dec |

Habitat and Distribution

The Common Blue occurs throughout the region in a variety of lowland grassland habitats, however it is most frequent along the coastal fringe and at urban locations. At urban sites it is typically associated with disturbed waste ground, including partially vegetated coal bings. The coal bing at Fallin, Stirlingshire and the waste ground at Stevenston, Ayrshire accommodated good numbers during the survey period.

The Common Blue tends to live in discrete colonies which at the best sites may contain several hundred adults. It favours short, flower-rich grassland, where the soil has low fertility, often with bare patches where the sun can form local hot spots. Pockets of taller grasses are also required as roost sites, where the adults rest head down on the grass flower heads in communal roosts. Although the majority of colonies are located on dry sites some areas of impeded drainage are also selected if Greater Birdsfoot-trefoil is present.

The Common Blue will avoid a dense sward or tall grassland. As a consequence of this some colonies survive for only a few years on disturbed ground and disappear when the grassland becomes too dense or when scrub invades. Fortunately, egg laying females can disperse over a wide area and newly formed habitats can be quickly colonised.

Status

A locally common butterfly that requires a succession of disturbed sites or managed grassland. At coastal locations the population is relatively stable and not of conservation concern. With the recent boom in the housing market, some colonies at urban waste ground sites have been lost as waste ground has been built on to meet the need for housing. This has particularly occurred in Dunbartonshire, and some of the colonies at Stevenston are likely to be lost to a large housing development.

Holly Blue *Celastrina argiolus*

Female on Holly, a caterpillar foodplant

Identification

This is the only blue butterfly apart from the Common Blue, likely to be found in the area. The male Holly Blue has all blue upperwings. The female is similar, but has black wing tips, the black becoming more extensive in the second generation. Both sexes normally hold their wings closed but do open them slightly in sunny weather to gain warmth. They rarely fully open their wings like the Common Blue.

The pale blue undersides of the wings with a speckling of small black dots distinguish the Holly Blue from the similar Common Blue, which has orange markings on the undersides. It could however be confused with the underside of the Small Blue, which used to occur in places where the Holly Blue is now found.

The Holly Blue's flight is stronger and more active than the Common Blue as they fly amongst the trees, shrubs and along hedgerows.

Life Cycle

The Holly Blue appears to have two broods in South West Scotland and has been recorded in late April/May and in July/August. The white eggs are typically laid on the flower buds of Holly in spring and on Ivy in summer. Several other caterpillar food plants are used elsewhere in Britain, such as Dogwood and Gorse (Emmet & Heath 1990) and Cotoneaster (Willmott 1999), and may also be used here. The caterpillar develops quickly while feeding on the flower buds. The Holly Blue over-winters as a chrysalis.

Holly Blue caterpillars are attacked by the host specific parasitic ichneumonid wasp *Listrodromus nycthemerus* and this is thought to be one of the reasons for fluctuations in its population size from year to year elsewhere in the UK. However, it is not yet clear if this parasite is present in the South West Scotland populations.

DISTRIBUTION

ABUNDANCE

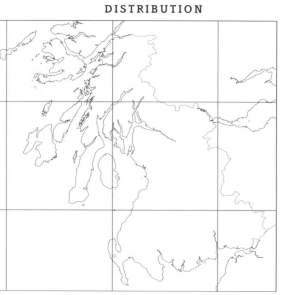

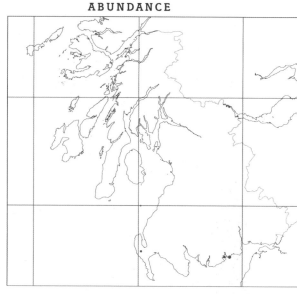

Holly Blue 1995-2004

| Jan | Feb | Mar | Apr | May | Jun | Jul | Aug | Sep | Oct | Nov | Dec |

Habitat and Distribution

The Holly Blue prefers woodland edges, hedgerows and parks and gardens that provide the caterpillar food plants, together with trees and shrubs that the adult butterflies visit to feed on aphid honey dew deposits on the leaves. The butterfly will also nectar on flowers, with Ragwort and Bramble being favourites.

Apart from a single record from Knapdale Forest in Argyll in 1972 (Thomson, 1980), all records are from Dumfries & Galloway. Thomson also notes one 18th century record for the species from Moffat. It was then unknown in Scotland until a single female was captured in Dumfries in 1950 by David Cunningham (Cunningham, 1950), who also saw one in the same area in 1973. All recent records of the Holly Blue are from sites along the Solway coast.

Since 1980, the butterfly has been recorded several times at Rockcliffe (NX8553). It was confirmed breeding for the first time in a garden there in 2004, and there were several other sightings nearby. In 2005 it was again recorded in Rockcliffe and at two locations in nearby Kippford (NX8354, NX8356 D. Welham pers.obs. on 14th May; A. White pers.obs.). It has also been recorded at Garlieston in 1990, and Dunskey, near Portpatrick (NX0155) in 2003 (G. Thomson pers.com.). There was a possible, but so far unconfirmed sighting at Rascarrel (NX8148) in 2003.

Status

The Holly Blue may have been misidentified as a Small Blue in the past, and have actually been more widespread than records suggest. It is therefore not certain if the Holly Blue has been present in very low numbers in Dumfries & Galloway for a long time, or if it is really a recent coloniser. Whatever its origin, with a generally warmer climate an expansion in the range of the Holly Blue would be predicted. It is worth looking out for anywhere along the Solway coast.

Identification

The Red Admiral is a magnificent insect, resplendent in red and black. The forewing tip is patterned with white spots and, at the base of the upper hindwings are small eye spots of the brightest blue. When the wings are closed and the butterfly is at rest the forewing is partially hidden behind the hindwing which is predominantly brown, but very attractive and well camouflaged, resembling a dead leaf. Both sexes are similar although the female is generally larger and less black than the male, being a very dark brown. The Red Admiral is a superb flyer and very fast and can flash past an observer when it is flying on a direct migratory route.

Life Cycle

Although the majority of Red Admiral butterflies seen in South West Scotland are European migrants their numbers are augmented by home grown butterflies. Females will lay a single green egg on a Stinging Nettle, that does not need to be part of a large patch but must have strong, healthy growth and be in the full sun. The caterpillar lives within a succession of leaves that it has loosely wrapped around itself with silk threads to from a leaf tent. The caterpillar emerges to feed on the leaf. When large and nearing maturity the caterpillar may move near to the top of the nettle, bite the stem, which causes the plant tip to fall allowing it to make a tent amongst the tip leaves in which to conceal itself (see Tucker M., 1997 for an excellent description of larval behaviour and life cycle). The chrysalis can be formed within a tent of leaves or away from the nettle patch on a plant stem. The chrysalis is an object of beauty being decorated with several gold patches. The chrysalis matures quickly and the adult butterfly hatches after about three weeks.

DISTRIBUTION

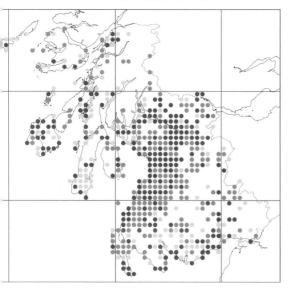

ABUNDANCE

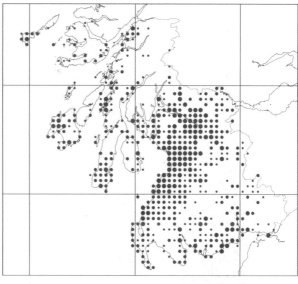

Red Admiral 1995-2004

Jan	Feb	Mar	Apr	May	Jun	Jul	Aug	Sep	Oct	Nov	Dec

Habitat and Distribution

Widespread as a migratory species the Red Admiral could be expected to be seen anywhere in South West Scotland, from garden to mountain slope and throughout the year from April to November.

It is most commonly seen in parks and gardens, particularly in August, September and October when it nectars on plants such as Buddleia and Michaelmas Daisy. Indeed, as many as fifty or so individuals can be clustered around a patch of Michaelmas Daisies during early autumn. When a good nectaring site has been found, such as a flower-rich garden, individuals tend to linger at the same spot for several days. A garden with fruit trees can be a further attraction as they feed on the sugars of rotting fruit, such as plums that have fallen to the ground.

Status

The Red Admiral is a widespread summer migrant, able to produce a brood but usually unable to survive our winter. In southern England there are recent records of over-wintering Red Admirals. Several records in April in South West Scotland, for example in 1995 at Muirkirk, Ayrshire (D. Galbraith), St. Johns Town of Dalry, Kirkcudbrightshire (J. Watson), Strathaven, Lanarkshire (A. Gunning), Fintry, Stirlingshire (P. Blount) and from Ailsa Craig on 21 April 1987 (Zonfrillo & Hancock 2004) may also have come from individuals that had successfully over-wintered in a building or sheltered place.

Painted Lady *Vanessa cardui*

Identification

A striking, large butterfly with the upper wing surfaces of both sexes patterned in orange, black and white. The undersides are equally beautiful with intricate patterns of orange and brown between the venation and blue eye spots on the hindwing. The Painted Lady is a large butterfly although it can vary in size with some home-grown individuals being two-thirds the size of a migrant butterfly. It is a fast and agile flyer and will visit Buddleia and other garden flowers to fuel its energetic, migratory urge.

Life Cycle

In South West Scotland the majority of sightings of the Painted Lady are migrants originating from North Africa, Europe and England with a peak in numbers during the late summer months of August and September. During years when the Painted Lady is common (such as 1996) the greenish eggs may be laid singly on thistles (*Cirsium* spp. and *Carduus* spp.). At Ledaig Nursery, Loch Creran, Argyll in 1996, sixty developing larvae were found on Marsh Cudweed (*Gnaphalium fuliginous*), a very unusual foodplant (J. MacKay pers.obs.). Stinging Nettle may also be used as a foodplant.

The caterpillar typically lives in a tent of thistle leaves spun together with silk, feeding on the leaves within the tent shelter. The chrysalis may be formed within the tent of leaves and the butterfly emerges after a period of about three weeks to join the migratory population.

DISTRIBUTION

ABUNDANCE

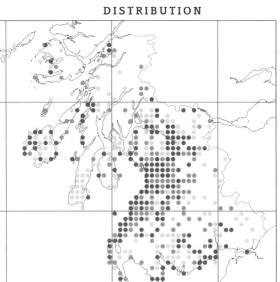

Painted Lady 1995-2004

| Jan | Feb | Mar | Apr | May | Jun | Jul | Aug | Sep | Oct | Nov | Dec |

Habitat and Distribution

As a migrant the Painted Lady could be found anywhere in South West Scotland but it has a tendency to favour the coastal fringe, urban waste ground, parks and gardens. These habitats provide a combination of warmth and flowering plants, such as Buddleia, Lesser Knapweed and Creeping Thistle which meet the nectar requirements of this itinerant butterfly.

Status

Unable to survive the winter the Painted Lady is an unpredictable migrant with some years providing many sightings, rarely an abundance, but more typically a series of occasional glimpses throughout the summer months. Some years, such as 2005 produce virtually no records.

Identification

Commonly encountered in gardens, the Small Tortoiseshell is one of our most familiar butterflies. Both sexes are similar in appearance with orange-brown upper surfaces with black and yellow stripes on the forewing and blue markings at the outer edges of both wings. Freshly emerged females can be identified from their swollen, egg-laden abdomens. When the wings are closed they are beautifully camouflaged as the dark brown under surfaces look like dead leaves.

Life Cycle

A mass of green eggs are laid together on Stinging Nettle, usually during May. The female selects egg laying sites carefully and will generally only lay eggs on large patches of nettles that are in the full sun. A small nettle patch, or nettles in the shade will be avoided. The young caterpillars emerge and stay together in a loose silk tent. As the caterpillars get larger they move away from the protective tent and feed on nettle leaves as solitary individuals. The mature caterpillars are very conspicuous as they feed near the top of the nettle and bask in the warmth of the sun. The chrysalis is formed in June on dead vegetation and adults emerge in July.

Adult butterflies are often found busily feeding on garden flowers such as Buddleia, Michaelmas Daisy and Ice Plant 'Autumn Joy', or on Creeping Thistle or Ragwort in the countryside. The nectar is consumed to provide energy for flight as they are highly mobile butterflies. During late summer a feeding frenzy occurs on any suitable flower to accumulate reserves to enable survival when it hibernates during the winter. Hibernation sites are often sheds, buildings, lofts and holes in trees. An adult butterfly can sometimes be seen in the winter when it has become disturbed during its winter rest, especially on warm days.

Small Tortoisehell

DISTRIBUTION

Small Tortoisehell

ABUNDANCE

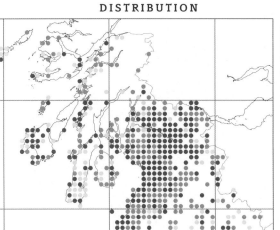

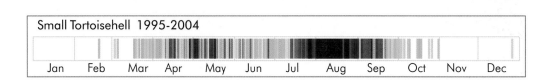

Small Tortoisehell 1995-2004

| Jan | Feb | Mar | Apr | May | Jun | Jul | Aug | Sep | Oct | Nov | Dec |

Habitat and Distribution

In South West Scotland the Small Tortoiseshell is widely distributed but numbers fluctuate and in some years very few are seen. It is most commonly seen in parks and gardens, coastal areas and woodland edges which support a rich array of flowers.

In the wider countryside large patches of Creeping Thistle may attract Small Tortoiseshells as this is a particularly favoured nectar source. In damper areas Hemp Agrimony is another preferred flower. The general tidying of the countryside and the destruction of patches of Creeping Thistle and Stinging Nettles may be contributing to a general reduction in the numbers seen.

Status

Although numbers fluctuate the Small Tortoiseshell has currently a relatively stable population in South West Scotland, with a widespread distribution and is currently not of conservation concern. Despite this it is often easy to become complacent when evaluating the status of a familiar butterfly. Some years have produced very low numbers of Small Tortoiseshell and it is not clear why. The caterpillar stage may be susceptible to disease as a result of wet summers, or parasitism may be a factor, and when this is combined with the general decline in suitable patches of Stinging Nettle in the wider countryside this may explain the low numbers.

Identification

A large and familiar garden butterfly, irresistibly attracted to Buddleia flowers. The Peacock is one of our most colourful butterflies with prominent eye-spots on the upper wing surfaces. Both sexes are similar and the eye-spot coloration serves two functions, to startle and to prevent a fatal attack to the body. When at rest the wings are closed and the butterfly appears dark brown or black due to the dark colouration of the wing undersides. If the butterfly is disturbed by a potential predator it opens its wings to reveal the brightly coloured eye spots, and the startled predator may then back away. In the case of a bird attack the bird may peck at a wing eye spot instead of pecking at the vulnerable body, allowing the butterfly to escape with a damaged wing.

Life Cycle

The Peacock shares a similar life cycle to the Small Tortoiseshell. The female lays green eggs as a mass on the leaves of Stinging Nettles in early summer. Like the Small Tortoiseshell the female Peacock will usually only lay eggs on a large nettle patch which is in full sun. The young caterpillars stay together in a protective silken tent and then disperse when nearing maturity to feed solitarily within the nettle patch. The mature caterpillar is large in size and a glistening black with many spines. The chrysalis is often formed on the nettle, close to where it fed as a caterpillar. The peak emergence is in August and the butterfly will then continue to fly until temperatures cool. It will then hibernate in winter to fly again in the spring when temperatures rise.

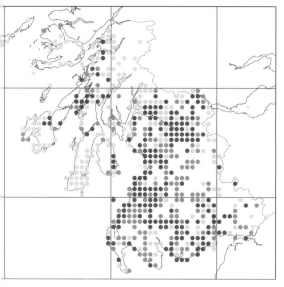

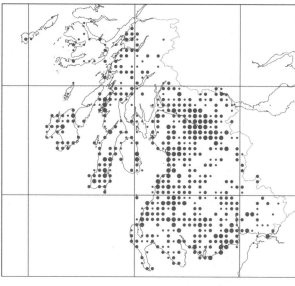

Peacock 1995-2004

| Jan | Feb | Mar | Apr | May | Jun | Jul | Aug | Sep | Oct | Nov | Dec |

Habitat and Distribution

Although most commonly seen in parks and gardens and coastal areas, it also frequents woodland glades and flower-rich meadows where the flowers of Lesser Knapweed and thistles are especially favoured as nectar sources.

The Peacock is a resident species in South West Scotland. It declined in the 1980s and early 1990s but since 1996 has made a dramatic comeback and has been expanding its range and is now widespread throughout the branch area.

In Dunbartonshire the Peacock was uncommon and absent from large areas but during 2002 and 2003 it spread throughout the vice-county and it is now established as a widespread resident breeding species. In 2004 the Peacock did particularly well with large numbers of butterflies recorded from many areas of South West Scotland. The home bred population is also augmented by migrants from other parts of Britain and Europe.

Status

As a widespread species and a butterfly that is increasing in range and abundance the Peacock is currently not a species of conservation concern in South West Scotland. Indeed, this is possibly another example of a butterfly species that has increased its range as a result of several recent warm years, in particular the milder winters leading to an increase in the survival of over-wintering butterflies.

Identification

Named for the white comma mark on the underside of the hindwing, the Comma is an attractive butterfly with upperwings having black marks on a warm orange-brown background. The Comma is easily identified by the ragged outline of the wing edge, which provides camouflage when the wings are closed, as the brown shading on the outer wings resembles a dead leaf. Both sexes are similar in appearance although males tend to be slightly smaller and have a more ragged wing edge. The antennae are particularly conspicuous being long and rigid with white tips.

Life Cycle

In South West Scotland there have been too few observations of the Comma to describe the life cycle in detail. As in England and Wales, mated females would be expected to lay the green-brown coloured eggs singly on Stinging Nettle, the preferred larval food plant. The Hop, an alternative food plant in England and Wales, is rare in South West Scotland. The Wych Elm, another possible foodplant is widespread in Scotland. The caterpillar lives as a solitary individual and does not form a leaf tent. The mature caterpillar is attractively marked, having a white patch on the rear of the body, providing a resemblance to a bird dropping. The chrysalis is usually formed on the nettle patch or adjacent vegetation near the ground close to dead shrivelled leaves. Two broods are normally produced in England and Wales, with the first brood butterflies being paler than the second brood. Males are highly territorial and will investigate any passing butterfly and then return to a favoured perch if a female is not encountered. They typically rest with a flat posture with wings held wide open.

The adult butterfly over-winters and it is during this period that the camouflage and resemblance to a dead leaf is important for its survival. It is quite possible that adults successfully over-winter in South West Scotland and the recent number of mild winters in southern Scotland may have facilitated the recent colonisation.

Comma

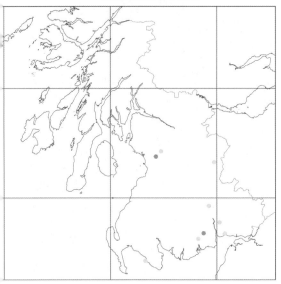

Comma

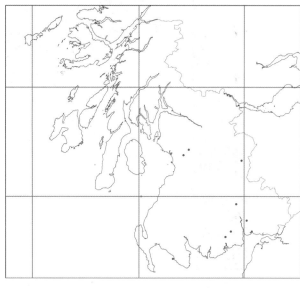

Comma 1995-2004											
Jan	Feb	Mar	Apr	May	Jun	Jul	Aug	Sep	Oct	Nov	Dec

Habitat and Distribution

The consistent number of sightings of the Comma during the recording period may be of migratory individuals from Northern England. It is however thought that as the Comma has also been seen in the Borders and the Lothians, and in greater numbers than in South West Scotland, that the Comma has begun to successfully colonise southern Scotland as a whole.

A scatter of records were received from Dumfries & Galloway, Ayrshire and Lanarkshire but it could be expected anywhere in South West Scotland at the preferred habitats of woodland glades, mature hedgerows and large gardens. An early record of 11th April, in 2001, suggests that the Comma may have successfully over-wintered.

Status

At present the northwards push in the distribution of the Comma marks an exciting development in the Lepidoptera fauna of South West Scotland and southern Scotland generally. If the trend of mild winters continue, the Comma would be expected to consolidate in numbers and then become more common and widespread.

Mating pair, the female is on the right

Identification

A beautiful butterfly with orange and black upperwings and a chequered pattern of white, orange and brown on the undersides. Newly emerged butterflies may have a greenish tinge on their body and wing base. The female is larger than the male, has darker margins to the upper forewings and has more white on the underside of the hindwing. The *insularum* subspecies, which occurs in South West Scotland, is particularly bright with large white markings. The two innermost patches of white on the underwings, near the wing base, are smaller in the male when compared to the female. Both sexes have deep blue eyes.

Life Cycle

The Small Pearl-bordered Fritillary is single brooded flying from late May to early August, and occasionally into September. The males are more active than females and actively seek out mating and nectaring opportunities. An egg-laden female has a swollen abdomen and prefers to crawl around. It will climb up a grass or rush stem to gain height and then launch into flight. The pale straw coloured eggs are laid singly on Marsh Violet leaves at wetter sites and on Common Dog Violet at drier sites. There is also some evidence which suggests that Wild Pansy has been used at one site in Glasgow (R. Sutcliffe pers.obs.). The caterpillar hatches in mid-summer and actively feeds on violet leaves until early autumn when it over-winters in the leaf litter. The following spring sees a resumption in feeding on violet leaves. The mature caterpillar is brown-black with many spines. In early May it forms a chrysalis, suspended on vegetation just above ground level.

Small Pearl-bordered
Fritillary

DISTRIBUTION

Small Pearl-bordered
Fritillary

ABUNDANCE

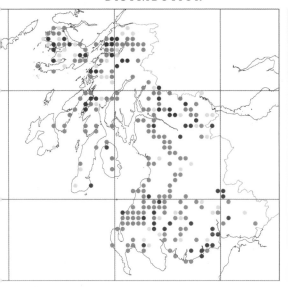

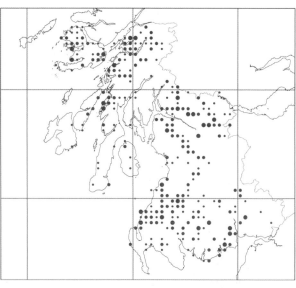

Small Pearl-bordered Fritillary 1995-2004											
Jan	Feb	Mar	Apr	May	Jun	Jul	Aug	Sep	Oct	Nov	Dec

Habitat and Distribution

The Small Pearl-bordered Fritillary is sensitive to habitat succession. It favours sheltered, open, sunny areas that tend to be wet, receive mineral enrichment from flushing, or run-off, that allows a vigorous growth of Marsh Violets. These pockets of habitat also typically accommodate the Marsh Thistle, a favoured source of nectar. In Dunbartonshire the Small Pearl-bordered Fritillary has successfully colonised many young coniferous plantations. The fritillary colony builds in numbers until the trees mature and shade out the habitat. But as long as a series of clearings are retained and provided, either by selective felling, accidental fire or the establishment of fire breaks, the fritillary can survive by moving along rides from one open area to another.

In addition to open coniferous and broad-leaved woodland the fritillary can also colonise grassland and moorland providing there is wind shelter, warmth from the sun and a lush growth of either Marsh Violet or Common Dog Violet.

Status

The Small Pearl-bordered Fritillary is widespread in South West Scotland and the population here represents a major British stronghold. There have been local declines, for example in Glasgow but there have also been increases in its distribution, for example in Dunbartonshire.

At some sites such as the woodlands in Argyll, Dunbartonshire and Dumfries & Galloway this fritillary is locally common, and over much of its range in South West Scotland it appears to be stable. However, because of recent severe declines elsewhere in the UK it is listed in several Local Biodiversity Action Plans, including those for Glasgow, East Dunbartonshire and North Lanarkshire for local conservation action.

Identification

The Pearl-bordered Fritillary is the earliest flying fritillary in Scotland with an emergence in late April and early May. Distinguishing between the Small Pearl-bordered Fritillary and Pearl-bordered Fritillary is often difficult but they can be easily separated when the undersides of the hindwings are seen close up. The Pearl-bordered Fritillary has only two central pearl markings with a generally pale golden coloured background. The Small Pearl-bordered Fritillary however shows seven or eight central patches of silver-white, with more contrasting pale and brown markings. Both species have similar orange and black upperwings.

The adult butterfly flies with short gliding interludes near to the ground. It is attracted to a wide range of early spring flowers including Bugle, Dandelion, Birdsfoot-trefoil and Bluebell.

Life Cycle

The Pearl-bordered Fritillary is single brooded with a relatively short flight period, flying in May to mid June. It breeds in colonies or in linked sub-colonies whose exact location may change from year to year due to their dependence on early spring successional vegetation. Females lay their pale yellow eggs amongst either Common Dog Violet or Marsh Violet that are growing profusely in a warm site with a sheltered south-facing aspect. Preferred areas often have little other vegetation but do have bare ground or shallow Bracken litter retaining warmth for egg and caterpillar development. The caterpillars feed intermittently on dense flushes of violet seedlings or the freshest foliage of established violets. During the winter they hibernate in curled up leaves amongst the litter, resuming feeding and basking in sunshine in March before pupating under violet leaves or in nearby vegetation.

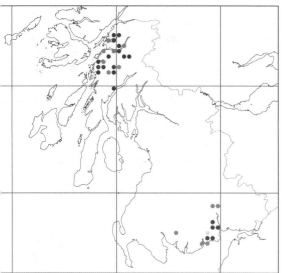

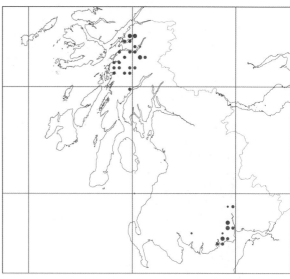

Pearl-bordered Fritillary	1995-2004										
Jan	Feb	Mar	Apr	May	Jun	Jul	Aug	Sep	Oct	Nov	Dec

Habitat and Distribution

The Pearl-bordered Fritillary is primarily a species of open woodland or mosaics of well drained grassland and Bracken and scrub where the Bracken mimics a woodland canopy by shading out grasses and allowing violets to thrive. Site management has a major influence on the survival of this species as their requirement for unshaded successional habitat means that some degree of disturbance or management is vital. This can be either by felling, coppicing, roadside management, Bracken management or light winter grazing by cattle. These management regimes maintain a continuity of suitable clearings that promote violet growth in sunny spots. The butterflies can follow the line of a sunny ride or path within a wood to a new suitable location but are unlikely to colonise an isolated site which makes them vulnerable to extinction.

Colonies vary in size from fewer than 20 adults to several thousand following forest clearance at a suitable site, before falling again as the breeding area becomes overgrown after 5-7 years. Careful habitat management and well designed felling and planting systems can support colonies through provision of a series of connected clearings. A good example of this management can be found at Lochaber Loch Forest Nature Reserve in Mabie Forest, near Dumfries. At this site, boundary banks and ditch edges are especially favoured if maintained as sheltered, unshaded habitat. It has been found that it is particularly beneficial to remove brash from such banks, following felling or scrub clearance as brash encourages Bramble and Gorse which inhibits violet colonisation.

Status

Nationally and in South West Scotland the Pearl-bordered Fritillary has suffered dramatic declines, due primarily to changes in the management of woodland and grassland. The main stronghold populations occur in Argyll. It has disappeared from central areas of Scotland and Ayrshire. In Dumfries & Galloway it has also declined and has contracted to a few core colonies, which are vulnerable but currently appear to be relatively stable. This is a species of conservation concern and is a high priority species for monitoring in our branch area due to the nationally significant populations.

Identification

The Dark Green Fritillary is the largest fritillary to be found in South West Scotland. It is a beautiful butterfly with the upperwings having black markings on an orange background. The underside of the wings have a greenish suffusion between silvery white spots which account for the name of the butterfly. The sexes are differently marked with the female having more defined black markings on the wing margins and being larger and paler orange. At some locations the *scotica* subspecies is found and both sexes have a greater amount of black on the upperwings and more green on the underwings. This is very conspicuous in females which in flight look very different and appear much darker than normal.

The Dark Green Fritillary can be a frustrating butterfly to watch, particularly the males as they are strong flyers and many sightings are of an orange blur passing by an observer as it fights against the wind. It is only when it settles to feed on a flower, often a Creeping Thistle, Spear Thistle or Lesser Knapweed, that the beauty of this butterfly can be seen.

Life Cycle

There is one brood in South West Scotland and the adult butterfly is on the wing between late June and mid-August, occasionally early September. The yellow eggs are laid singly on Marsh Violet at wet locations and on Common and Heath Dog Violets at drier sites. The caterpillar is long lived and is the over-wintering stage. It hibernates as a very small caterpillar soon after hatching from the egg in late summer. It emerges from leaf litter during the first warm days of spring to feed on violets. A large caterpillar when fully grown, it is velvety black with spines and a row of orange red spots low on the sides. The chrysalis is formed in May in a shelter of loosely spun leaves.

DISTRIBUTION

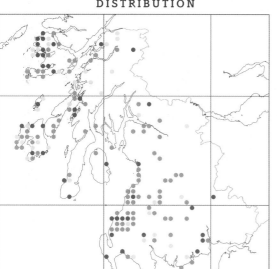

ABUNDANCE

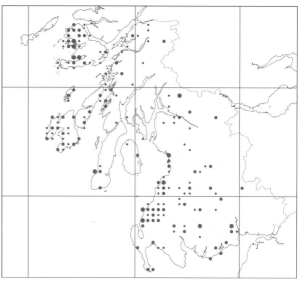

Dark Green Fritillary 1995-2004											
Jan	Feb	Mar	Apr	May	Jun	Jul	Aug	Sep	Oct	Nov	Dec

Habitat and Distribution

The Dark Green Fritillary occupies two distinct habitat types in South West Scotland. It is either found along the coast, amongst dunes with grassland and pockets of woodland, or in upland wooded glens with open areas of wet grassland that receive the full warmth of the sun.

The coastal areas of Dumfries & Galloway, South Ayrshire and Argyll together with a few inland glens support the majority of the Dark Green Fritillaries in South West Scotland. It has a widespread distribution but when encountered it is often seen in small numbers, frequently as a solitary male which can be highly mobile and cover large distances.

Status

The Dark Green Fritillary is a local, but widespread butterfly and generally uncommon, rarely found in large numbers. There appears to be a recent decline in records, particularly along the coast in Dumfries & Galloway and Ayrshire. Although currently not a species of conservation concern, regular monitoring is required to determine the stability of the population and the extent of recent declines.

Marsh Fritillary *Euphydryas aurina*

A male Marsh Fritillary (Taynish NNR) –
a beautiful butterfly that is vulnerable and
requiring careful monitoring

Identification

The Marsh Fritillary is the most brightly
marked of our fritillaries, with a
distinctive chequered pattern of yellow
and orange patches on the upperwings
and a pale underside with a beautiful
pattern of orange and pale spots. The
legs, head palps and underside of the
antennae are a distinctive ginger-
orange. The upperwing pattern and
colour can be variable and some
individuals have more extensive black
markings. The sexes are similar,
although the female tends to be slightly
paler and is larger in size, often
recognised by a swollen, egg-laden
abdomen. When fresh the Marsh
Fritillary is a very attractive butterfly but
the wings are fragile and they soon get
damaged.

Life Cycle

The flight period is short from late May
to early July in a single brood. Large
batches of yellow-orange eggs are laid on
prominent Devil's-bit Scabious plants or
in patches of vegetation where this food
plant is abundant, in a warm sunny
situation. The black caterpillars are
gregarious and spin a conspicuous
protective web. They over-winter in the
web, close to the ground, emerging to
bask in the early spring sunshine. As they
grow they disperse in search of food and
feed as solitary individuals. Pupation
normally takes place in late April and
early May, deep within grassy tussocks or
dead leaves. Males emerge first and
search for females in a low zigzagging
flight. Females are often so heavy with
eggs that they crawl across the vegetation
in search of a suitable laying site rather
than expend too much energy flying.

Marsh Fritillary

DISTRIBUTION

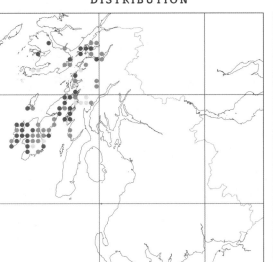

Marsh Fritillary

ABUNDANCE

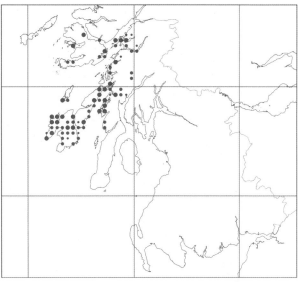

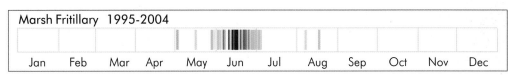

Marsh Fritillary 1995-2004											
Jan	Feb	Mar	Apr	May	Jun	Jul	Aug	Sep	Oct	Nov	Dec

Habitat and Distribution

The Marsh Fritillary is a species of herb-rich, wet acid grassland that is lightly grazed, with an abundance of Devil's-bit Scabious. It forms compact colonies on small patches of marshy grassland habitat that are warmed by the sun, often with adjacent scrub that provides wind shelter. This fritillary is renowned for large cyclical fluctuations in population size. At Taynish NNR (NR7385) peak butterfly counts have occurred in the years 1978, 1985, 1991, 1997 and 2005 which suggests an approximate 7 year cycle (John Halliday pers.com.). The caterpillars may be parasitized by *Cotesia melitaearum* wasps but it is unclear if the parasites are responsible for fluctuations in population size. During low count periods colonies are prone to local extinction, but they can quickly recover to colonise nearby suitable habitat in good years and contract to core colonies in poor years. A patchwork of suitable habitat over a large area is therefore an essential requirement for the survival of this species.

Scottish populations now seem to be confined to Argyll. Colonies are found in mainland Argyll from West Loch Tarbert on the Kintyre peninsula in the south, to Glen Creran in the north, and on the islands of Islay, Jura, Colonsay, Mull and Lismore. There are no recent records from Central Scotland or Dumfries & Galloway.

Status

The Marsh Fritillary in South West Scotland represents one of the stronghold populations in Britain, and indeed in Europe. It is a species that is vulnerable and has declined in many areas of Britain and it is a protected species. The main threats to this beautiful butterfly are from agricultural intensification, drainage of unintensified grassland, overgrazing and afforestation. This is a priority species for monitoring to ensure that the South West Scotland populations remain, due to its high national and international importance. Further research is also required on the effects of parasites on the Argyll population.

A Speckled Wood of the subspecies *oblita* (Isle of Jura, Argyll)

Identification

A medium sized dark brown butterfly with a dappling of pale yellow or white patches on the upperwings. The Argyll Speckled Wood butterflies are of the *oblita* subspecies and are generally larger than the English counterparts, and have larger spots although markings and colour can be variable and vary between broods. A freshly emerged Speckled Wood with wings open in the full sun has an oily sheen to the wings which adds to their beauty. Some individuals are particularly dark being almost black.

The females tend to be larger than males and have larger yellow-white spots on their wings otherwise they are very similar to males. The males frequently bask in the sun with wings held wide open.

Life Cycle

The butterfly is on the wing from late April to September and there are at least two broods. The pale yellow eggs are laid on a variety of grasses including Cock's-foot and Couch grass. The over-wintering stage can either be a caterpillar or chrysalis. The pale green chrysalis either suspends from a stout grass blade or is hidden within a clump of vegetation.

Typical behaviour of the male is a quick, short burst of flight between shrubs or trees along a hedgerow or woodland edge resting at sunspots which are defended as temporary territories. An encounter between two males may lead to a spiral flight between the two until one male moves away. Whereas males are highly active the females usually spend more time near the tree canopy. Favoured trees include the Ash, Oak and Alder where both sexes feed on aphid honeydew deposits on the leaves.

DISTRIBUTION

ABUNDANCE

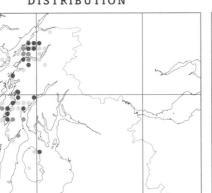

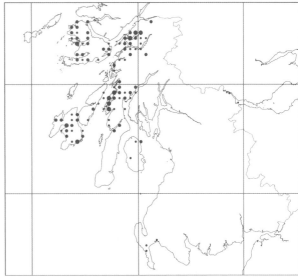

| Speckled Wood 1995-2004 |
| Jan | Feb | Mar | Apr | May | Jun | Jul | Aug | Sep | Oct | Nov | Dec |

Habitat and Distribution

The Speckled Wood has a puzzling distribution in South West Scotland. Despite plenty of suitable habitat throughout the area it is confined to Argyll, with a possible colonisation attempt in Dumfries & Galloway. In Argyll, the Speckled Wood is a butterfly of open woodland edges and glades where there are sun spots to bask in and for males to hold temporary territories. It is not clear why the distribution should be so restricted.

The origin of the individual Speckled Wood butterflies recorded in Dumfries & Galloway from Kirkmadrine, Stoneykirk and Torrs Warren in the 1990s is unclear and may possibly be from the nearby population from Northern Ireland.

Status

The Speckled Wood appears to be slowly increasing its distribution in South West Scotland and it is one of the species that would be expected to increase in range as the climate warms. The possible colonisation attempt in Dumfries & Galloway may reflect this trend.

A male Wall Brown in a typical posture of open wings, on the ground, basking in sunshine

Identification

A medium sized orange and brown butterfly that loves to bask on open ground in full sun. The sexes are similar although the female is slightly larger, paler and lacks the dark sex-brand marking on the forewing of the male. The upperwings have conspicuous eye-spots and when at rest with wings closed it also shows an eye-spot on the underside forewing, distinctive of all the Brown family. The underside hindwing of the Wall Brown is a beautiful pattern of circles and wavy lines which enhance the camouflage when the wings are closed.

Life Cycle

There are two generations, with the adults flying from mid-May to late June and again from early August into September. The males are short lived and can be highly active as they patrol a territory in search of a female between bouts of sun basking. The female can often be seen basking on the ground in full sun but is generally less active than the male. The pale yellow eggs are laid singly on a variety of grasses, that include Cock's-foot and Yorkshire Fog. The green caterpillars are nocturnal feeders. The second brood caterpillars over-winter and resume feeding on grass leaves in the early spring before pupation in April.

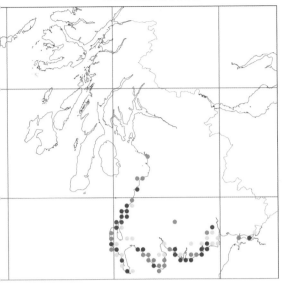

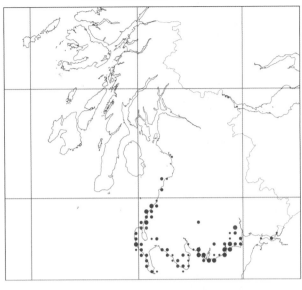

Wall Brown 1995-2004											
Jan	Feb	Mar	Apr	May	Jun	Jul	Aug	Sep	Oct	Nov	Dec

Habitat and Distribution

The Wall Brown favours open coastal grassland where the turf is patchy and broken by bare soil or stones that heat quickly from the sun.

It is at the northern limit of its British distribution in South West Scotland and is currently restricted to the coastal fringe of Dumfries & Galloway and South Ayrshire, with the occasional site found inland, for example at Mabie Forest (NX 9270).

At Mabie Forest it was first recorded on a butterfly transect walk in 1997 during late spring. During 1998 one was recorded in spring and summer, in 1999 two were recorded in spring and 25 in summer. The Wall Brown is now well established in both transects undertaken at Mabie (J. MacKay pers.obs.).

Status

The Wall Brown appears to have a stable or increasing population in South West Scotland which is a contrast to many other parts of Britain where it has recently declined.

If the trend of mild winters continues it would be expected that the Wall Brown will expand its distribution further north and colonise other coastal areas. The occasional record, for example from Dumbarton in 1990 (K. Futter pers.obs.), before the atlas survey recording period, would indicate that there is potential for expansion in the range of the Wall Brown in South West Scotland.

Mountain Ringlet *Erebia epiphron*

Mating pair, female is above the male

Identification

A small dark brown butterfly that has orange and black eye-spots merging as bands on both upper and underwing surfaces. Both sexes are similar although the female is larger and a paler brown than the male. Some males are very dark, appearing almost black. The swollen abdomen of an egg-laden female is also a conspicuous feature. The *scotica* subspecies is generally larger and more brightly coloured than the Mountain Ringlet found in the Lake District. A noticeable feature of the Mountain Ringlet is the white legs and white antennae which contrast strongly against the dark wings.

A newly emerged male can be a very active butterfly as it seeks out a female but flight only occurs in sunshine. In shady, cool conditions the butterflies conserve energy and rest among grasses and become difficult to find.

Life Cycle

Adult butterflies live for only a few days and the flight period as a whole is short from late June to early August. As a mountain butterfly the climate plays an important role in flight times and general behaviour, and energy conservation seems to be important. When a male finds a female there is no elaborate courtship but just a simple pairing in the grass. Mated females are less active than males, generally conserving energy and being less conspicuous to bird predators such as the Meadow Pipit. The pale yellow eggs are laid singly near the ground, often on dead grass blades of Mat-grass or Sheep's Fescue. The caterpillar emerges in late July and early August. The main food plant is thought to be Mat-grass but it is possible that other grasses and sedges may be eaten, particularly Sheep's Fescue and Common Bent which occur alongside Mat-grass (see Holland, 2000). The caterpillar is a nocturnal feeder and feeds on the grass blade tips before hiding at the grass base during the day. The immature caterpillar hibernates in late August and September and survives the winter frost and snow to emerge in the spring to start feeding again. It is thought that it may take the caterpillar two years to mature at some sites depending on climate conditions. The mature caterpillar pupates at the base of grasses in late May or June.

Mountain Ringlet

DISTRIBUTION

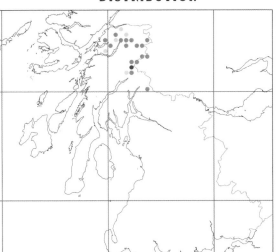

Mountain Ringlet

ABUNDANCE

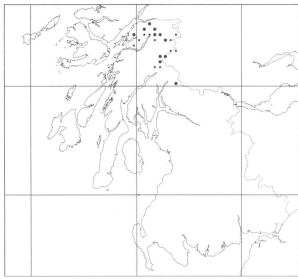

Mountain Ringlet 1995-2004											
Jan	Feb	Mar	Apr	May	Jun	Jul	Aug	Sep	Oct	Nov	Dec

Habitat and Distribution

The Mountain Ringlet is the only true mountain butterfly in Scotland, being found at an altitude of 350-1000m. It is also occasionally seen close to sea level (J. Halliday pers.com.). It may however fly alongside the Small Heath which can also survive at moderately high altitudes. Favoured habitats of the Mountain Ringlet are wet, flushed grassland on sloping ground that is normally south facing and lightly grazed, although the fenced enclosure at Ben Lawers Nature Reserve prevents grazing and supports the butterflies. The flushing at these habitats promotes a lush growth of grass amongst sedges and rushes. The adult butterfly occasionally nectars on the flowers available such as Tormentil, Heath Spotted Orchid, Cross-leaved Heath, Heath Bedstraw and Valerian.

The population stronghold is located at the Breadalbane mountain range that passes from Argyll, through Stirlingshire and into Highland Region and Perthshire. The colony on Ben Lomond beside Loch Lomond is the most southerly site for the butterfly in Scotland.

Status

As a consequence of being a mountain species the colonies can become isolated and vulnerable to climate change and land management. Currently the range of Mountain Ringlet appears to be stable although the difficulties in recording mean that distribution maps may not be fully accurate.

The individual colonies in South West Scotland collectively represent an important population of the Mountain Ringlet and their biology and status require further investigation and monitoring.

A female Scotch Argus, *caledonia* subspecies

Identification

A beautiful butterfly with dark brown velvety wings interrupted by an orange band containing conspicuous eye spots. The Scotch Argus in South West Scotland is of the *caledonia* subspecies, which has a narrowing of the orange band on the upper forewing between the top two and bottom eyespots and rarely has more than three eye spots (see Thomson, 1980). The males are darker than females, sometimes almost black, and tend to be smaller but both sexes have similar upperwing markings. When freshly emerged they have a distinct white fringe to the wings. The underside of both the male and female are variable. The female has the lower hindwing as either pale yellow-brown or dark brown with a grey-violet band. The male hindwings can be a striking dark chocolate brown with a broad grey-violet band or paler brown.

When the sun shines the males fly low just above the grass tussocks on a constant search for females but as soon as the sun becomes clouded over the butterflies seek refuge in the grassy tussocks, to resume their flight again when the sun comes out. Females are less active, particularly when burdened by a heavy egg load but can be frequently seen nectaring on Marsh Thistle and other available flowers.

Life Cycle

The Scotch Argus has a short flight time from mid-July to early September with a peak in early August and there is one brood. The pale yellow eggs are laid singly on low-lying vegetation close to the ground. For example, eggs have been found on the flower stalk of low growing Tormentil (K. Futter pers.obs). Although Purple Moor-grass is the favoured food plant of the nocturnal caterpillar, other grasses may also be eaten such as Tufted Hair-grass, Wavy Hair-grass, Sheep's Fescue and Common Bent (Kirkland, 2005). The caterpillar is the over-wintering stage and resumes feeding in early spring until it is mature in late June or early July. Pupation takes place at the base of grass tussocks.

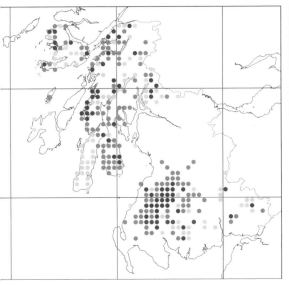

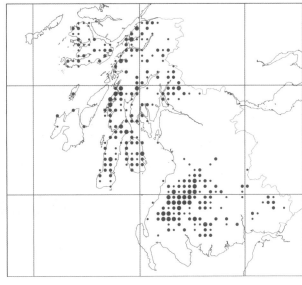

Scotch Argus 1995-2004

| Jan | Feb | Mar | Apr | May | Jun | Jul | Aug | Sep | Oct | Nov | Dec |

Habitat and Distribution

The Scotch Argus is typically found in discrete colonies in areas of suitable upland habitat, but these can merge to form a very large colony. For example, Glen Douglas in Dunbartonshire contains hundreds of individuals and the best sites in Argyll contain thousands. The preferred habitat is damp, lush open grassland often on a slope that receives mineral enrichment from flushing and is warmed by the full sun. Pockets of grassland that are colonised by Scotch Argus are typically sheltered by scrub or open woodland and only lightly grazed. Newly re-stocked conifer plantations can also provide a temporary habitat.

In Dunbartonshire Scotch Argus colonies are typically found where tussocks of Purple Moor-grass grow amongst Bog Myrtle. The Bog Myrtle may be important in providing cover for the developing caterpillar against predation. The wet acid upland grasslands favoured by the Scotch Argus tend to have few flowers but in areas of mineral flushing the variety of flowers increases and these sites will contain the highest density of butterflies. Nectaring opportunities are usually provided by Marsh Thistle, Heath

Spotted Orchid, Devil's-bit Scabious, Wild Angelica, Cross-leaved Heath and Heather but also by Lesser Knapweed and Ragwort at drier spots.

Where suitable habitat occurs the Scotch Argus is locally abundant and strong colonies are found in Dumfries & Galloway, South Ayrshire, Dunbartonshire and Argyll. The Scotch Argus habitats are typically at a higher altitude than those favoured by Meadow Brown or Ringlet but at intermediate altitudes all three species may fly together in the same patch of grassland, such as at Glen Luss and Glen Douglas, Dunbartonshire.

Status

In South West Scotland the Scotch Argus is not a species of conservation concern, but because of its limited distribution in Britain the colonies in South West Scotland are important. In its core areas, the Scotch Argus is often by far the most abundant butterfly. However, there is evidence of declines in the eastern and southern parts of its distribution in Scotland, but it is not clear whether this can be linked to warmer temperatures brought about by climate change, or changes to its habitats.

Grayling *Hipparchia semele*

The Grayling always rests with its wings closed, the eye spot shown here is normally hidden behind the hindwing

Identification

The Grayling is well camouflaged to blend into a background of rocky outcrops or stony ground and can be difficult to spot unless it moves. It has a rapid, distinctive bobbing and gliding flight. When it lands it sits with its wings closed and will usually tilt them over at an angle to the sun to regulate its temperature. If alarmed, or startled by another Grayling, it will flick its forewing upwards to reveal an orange patch with an eyespot.

The female is larger than the male and the upperwings are more brightly marked with orange which may be seen in flight. The orange areas have black eyespots with white pupils. The undersides of both sexes are similar, with cryptic markings but the colours are variable from pale grey to almost black.

Life Cycle

One of the later butterflies to emerge, Graylings are usually on the wing from late June until the end of August or early September. They are not often seen nectaring, but when they are, are often seen on Ragwort.

Eggs are usually laid singly on the blades of various grasses including Red Fescue and Tufted Hair-grass but are sometimes just laid on dead grass near the plants. The important requirement is for bare ground, in order to maintain a high enough temperature for the caterpillars to develop. The yellow and brown striped caterpillars feed at night at the tips of the grass blades. They overwinter as caterpillars and resume feeding in the spring, becoming fully grown in May or early June. They then pupate just below ground level.

Butterflies of South West Scotland

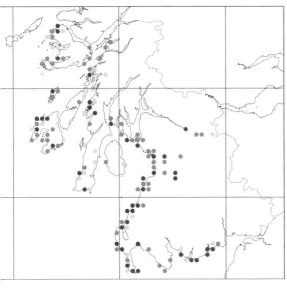

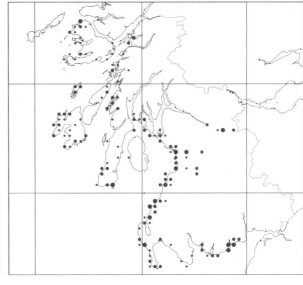

Grayling 1995-2004

| Jan | Feb | Mar | Apr | May | Jun | Jul | Aug | Sep | Oct | Nov | Dec |

Habitat and Distribution

The Grayling is rarely seen in large numbers, typically as an individual or a small group. It can be found at two different habitat types in South West Scotland, either at coastal locations or at industrial waste ground, so-called 'brownfield' sites.

The coastal habitats can be rocky cliffs, dunes, grassland, heathland or along woodland paths but all are characterised by having open bare areas of soil or stony ground that receive the full warmth of the sun. Along the coast of Dumfries & Galloway, Ayrshire and Argyll the Grayling is widespread but it is absent from the coasts of Inverclyde, Renfrewshire and Dunbartonshire, although an unconfirmed record was received of an individual Grayling observed in Helensburgh during 1997.

The brownfield sites are characterised by having bare areas of concrete, rubble, spoil and tarmac adjacent to grass and scrub. These areas heat up quickly and mimic stony and sandy coastal habitats. Brownfield sites such as those along the River Clyde from Glasgow to Motherwell, the former steelworks at Ravenscraig, Motherwell, and some Ayrshire sites at Kilmarnock and Stevenston hosted the Grayling during the survey period.

Status

Generally the Grayling has a relatively stable population along the coast and it is not a species of conservation concern although some Ayrshire sites have experienced local declines, particularly along the coast between Troon and Irvine.

On brownfield sites the Grayling is always under threat from the regeneration and development of the sites that it has occupied. In Glasgow the railway network and Clyde walkway provide a corridor route for the colonisation of suitable waste ground.

Female Meadow Brown

Identification

The Meadow Brown is a large, brown butterfly. The male is a darker brown and smaller than the female but otherwise they are similarly marked with both having an eye spot in an orange patch on the forewing. The female has more orange on the forewing and with age generally becomes a pale, fawn brown, as wing scales are lost. The colour of the eyes of some populations are slightly different between the sexes with the female having pale straw coloured eyes and the male having dark brown eyes.

The flight of the Meadow Brown is typically a gentle bobbing flight just above the grass stems or weaving between them and both sexes are active flyers. A freshly emerged male has tremendous stamina and will search relentlessly for a female amongst the grass.

The female Meadow Brown is larger than the male because during the period of time when copulating, and if disturbed, the female flies away carrying the joined male as a passive passenger and therefore requires greater flight capacity to carry the extra weight of the male.

Life Cycle

A single generation flies between June and September. The yellow-brown eggs are laid on a variety of grasses including Smooth Meadow-grass, Cock's-foot and Common Bent. The green caterpillar is usually a nocturnal feeder and grows slowly. It hibernates during the winter before resuming feeding in the spring. The chrysalis is formed near the ground, usually suspended from a grass stem, in May.

Meadow Brown

Meadow Brown

DISTRIBUTION

ABUNDANCE

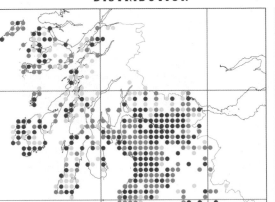
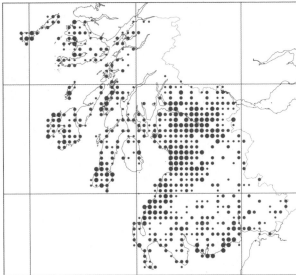

Meadow Brown	1995-2004										
Jan	Feb	Mar	Apr	May	Jun	Jul	Aug	Sep	Oct	Nov	Dec

Habitat and Distribution

Where there is a patch of lowland native grassland there is a good chance that a colony of the Meadow Brown butterfly will be found. In South West Scotland the Meadow Brown is second only to the Green-veined White in abundance and it is widely distributed. It is generally absent from sheep grazed hill sides, mountain slopes and wet heathland but can be found on drier moorland which have patches of ungrazed grassland.

It particularly favours flower-rich meadows, waste ground, coastal grassland and will venture into large gardens. In the wetter upland grassland habitats the Meadow Brown tends to be replaced by the Scotch Argus although the two species can be found alongside each other in some areas. In lowland wet grassland the Meadow Brown can be found alongside the Ringlet.

Male Meadow Brown

Status

The Meadow Brown is widespread and a relatively common butterfly in South West Scotland. As long as farming continues to become more wildlife-friendly, and semi-natural grasslands are not overgrazed or too regularly cut then the Meadow Brown will continue to be a familiar sight and not of conservation concern.

Ringlet on bramble, a favoured nectar source

Identification

Although predominantly dark brown the Ringlet is a very attractive butterfly when freshly emerged. The edges of the wings are fringed with white and the underwings have ringed eye-spots. Generally both sexes are similar in appearance although the male is slightly smaller and darker than the female. Variation includes the size of the ringed eye-spots, which can be small in the *parvipunctata* form and some populations have a grey-brown wing coloration.

Life Cycle

The Ringlet is on the wing from late June until mid-August. The male Ringlet is a butterfly on a mission being a very active butterfly as it bobs with a gentle flight between the grass stems looking for females. It will pause for a few seconds to get some warmth from the sun or re-fuel on nectar from a flower,

before setting off again to continue its search. The desire to find a mate is so strong that the male is one of the few butterflies that will fly in overcast weather and even during a bout of light rain. The Ringlet is also a peaceful butterfly. If two males come near to each other their flight direction is briefly interrupted and they then pass each other by and continue on their separate journeys without wasting energy on spiral flights.

After mating the female lays pale yellow eggs haphazardly amongst grasses. The pale yellow-brown caterpillar feeds on a variety of grasses such as Tufted Hair-grass and Cock's-foot. It is long-lived and is the over-wintering stage. It is a nocturnal feeder and takes nine to ten months to reach maturity before pupating. The pale brown chrysalis is formed near the ground in late spring, during late May and early June.

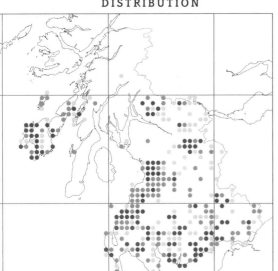

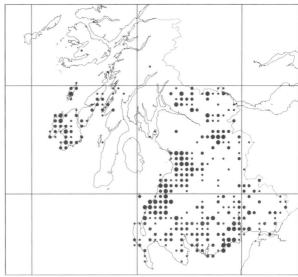

Ringlet 1995-2004

| Jan | Feb | Mar | Apr | May | Jun | Jul | Aug | Sep | Oct | Nov | Dec |

Habitat and Distribution

A butterfly of wet grasslands and woodland glades. In South West Scotland the Ringlet is scattered throughout although it is less widespread in Argyll. When the Glasgow Branch was formed in 1985, there was only one known colony in Lanarkshire (Cander Moss). It has recently increased its range, particularly in the Clyde and Avon river valleys in Lanarkshire (Futter, K. 1993) and in the wet grasslands of Dunbartonshire. A two pronged expansion in range from Lanarkshire, with butterflies moving north, and from Loch Lomond and the Kilpatricks, with butterflies moving south, has met in Glasgow, which now has many suitable grasslands occupied by the Ringlet.

The Ringlet may share the same habitat with the Meadow Brown, but generally prefers damper, lush grassland often at the edge of a woodland. In such habitats the Ringlet normally outnumbers the Meadow Brown. Occasionally Ringlets are also encountered in taller upland grassland habitats that have been protected from sheep grazing. In such habitats they can be found alongside Scotch Argus.

Status

During the recording period the Ringlet has been observed to expand its range dramatically in South West Scotland, particularly in Greater Glasgow. During 2005, outside the recording period of the atlas, further new records in Dunbartonshire, Renfrewshire, Glasgow, North Ayrshire and Argyll verify the continuing expansion in distribution. It is likely that the recent expansion in range will continue. It is currently not a species of conservation concern.

Mating pair on Harebell

Identification

A small orange-brown butterfly that can be easily overlooked. The sexes are similar in appearance with the female being slightly larger. When at rest or perching the wings are held shut and the inner orange wings are not shown. The eye-spot on the forewing is visible when newly perched or after landing on the ground. The Small Heath is an active butterfly and normally does not perch or rest for long. If the rest period is lengthy the forewing may be drawn down to hide the eye spot behind the hind wing and the butterfly then becomes very well camouflaged.

The Small Heath can vary in size and have local colour variation. In some upland areas, such as north Stirlingshire, it can be larger in size, particularly females, which have bright, almost luminous orange upperwings.

The Small Heath will usually fly away if disturbed, but in upland areas if it is cool weather and resting when disturbed it may draw its legs close to its body and feign death and drop from the piece of vegetation it was perched on in the manner of a dead leaf.

In flight the Small Heath has a lazy, bobbing flying action and normally hugs the ground particularly at coastal or waste ground sites or along paths such as forestry tracks. It often flies for a few metres and then lands on the ground. It then tilts its wings towards the sun to gain warmth in a similar manner to the Grayling.

Life Cycle

The Small Heath is usually single brooded in South West Scotland and it is most commonly seen on the wing during late May to early August. The males hold

Small Heath

DISTRIBUTION

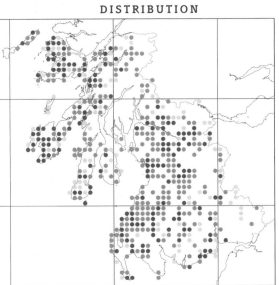

Small Heath

ABUNDANCE

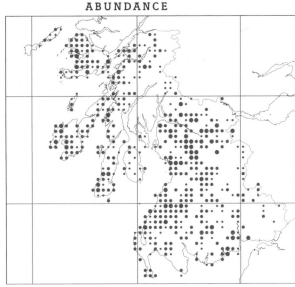

Small Heath 1995-2004											
Jan	Feb	Mar	Apr	May	Jun	Jul	Aug	Sep	Oct	Nov	Dec

small, loose territories and will chase away rival males in a spiral fight or intercept passing females and begin courtship. At upland sites the male Small Heath may fly just above the Heather, Blaeberry, grasses and rushes in a relatively confined territorial area.

The pale green eggs are laid on a variety of grasses especially fescues, such as Sheep's Fescue and Red Fescue. The green caterpillar is well camouflaged and is the over-wintering stage. It forms a chrysalis in early spring, attached to a grass stem.

Habitat and Distribution

The Small Heath is a widespread and a relatively common butterfly in South West Scotland although it is sensitive to changes in land management and habitat succession and it can quickly disappear from areas if they become unsuitable.

The butterfly is typically seen as a solitary individual or in small colonies. Larger colonies can however be found on upland grassland and hill slopes where the Small Heath can be the most common butterfly.

The Small Heath is found in a variety of vegetation types and is equally at home in both wet and dry habitats. In wet areas it can be found at a rush dominated marsh, upland heathland, hill side flushes and even some blanket bog sites were it will fly with the Large Heath. On mountain slopes it may fly alongside the Mountain Ringlet. At drier sites it will frequent coastal grasslands, countryside tracks and paths, urban waste ground and lowland grassland habitats where it may occur alongside the Meadow Brown. Despite having a fairly weak flight it can also be a highly mobile species and it will venture into gardens.

Status

Although numbers can fluctuate the Small Heath is a relatively common and widespread butterfly in South West Scotland and is currently not a species of conservation concern.

Large Heath *Coenonympha tullia*

Large Heath, *polydama* subspecies on Bell Heather

Identification

The Large Heath is a brown and orange butterfly intermediate in size between the Small Heath and Meadow Brown. Like the Small Heath it never opens its wings when at rest. In South West Scotland the sub species *polydama* is the most common and this grades to the *scotica* subspecies in north Argyll and local areas in Dunbartonshire and Stirlingshire. The *polydama* subspecies has orange brown coloured undersides with eye spots whereas *scotica* lacks the eye spots, is a paler orange and looks very similar to a large sized Small Heath.

The Large Heath has the same bobbing flight action of a Meadow Brown and weaves between or just above the heather and tussocks of Hare's-tail Cotton-grass, occasionally stopping to nectar from a flower, particularly Cross-leaved Heath.

Life Cycle

The adult emerges in mid-June and has a very short flight period which lasts about a month with very few individuals seen by late July and early August. The short flight time reflects the short life span of the adults which live for only a few days. The males emerge first and actively seek out females. The females are less active and spend long periods resting between bouts of egg-laying, to remain undetected from their main predator, the Meadow Pipit. The pale yellow eggs are laid singly on Hare's-tail Cotton-grass, the main caterpillar food plant. The caterpillar is long-lived and is the over-wintering stage. It continues to feed in early spring before pupating in May. The chrysalis is suspended from a grass stem.

Large Heath

DISTRIBUTION

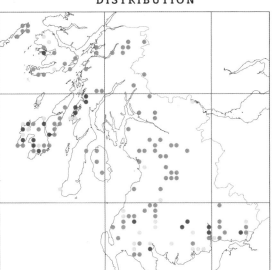

Large Heath

ABUNDANCE

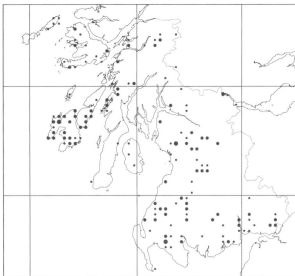

Large Heath 1995-2004

| Jan | Feb | Mar | Apr | May | Jun | Jul | Aug | Sep | Oct | Nov | Dec |

Habitat and Distribution

The preferred habitat of the Large Heath is lowland raised bogs and blanket bogs but it is also recorded from wet heathland.

The Large Heath is widespread in South West Scotland but will always have a scattered distribution due to the lack of suitable habitat in many areas.

The adults have poor dispersal rates and are rarely seen away from their breeding area. This makes the Large Heath a poor coloniser of nearby suitable habitat and is prone to local extinctions.

Fortunately some of the lowland raised bogs that support the Large Heath are Scottish Wildlife Trust reserves and sensitive management has encouraged the survival of this endangered butterfly.

Status

The preferred lowland bog habitats of the Large Heath are becoming increasingly isolated and threatened. Development from industry, housing, golf course development and recreation together with drainage and agricultural intensification are constant threats to the sensitive bog habitats remaining in South West Scotland. It is a sad fact that despite campaigns to save peatlands, they remain neglected and one of the most vulnerable habitats. There has been a general decline in recent records of the Large Heath and some colonies may have been lost. The Large Heath is a species of conservation concern in South West Scotland primarily because of the threats imposed on its habitat which threaten the stability of existing colonies. The threat to the Aucheninnes Moss in Dalbeattie to landfill, and Blackhill Mire, Helensburgh, Dunbartonshire from a golf course development are two examples of Large Heath colonies under threat.

Occasional Visitors and Recently Extinct Butterflies

Three species were recorded during the survey period as irregular, occasional visitors to South West Scotland. These were the Brimstone (*Gonepteryx rhamni*), Camberwell Beauty (*Nymphalis antiopa*) and the Monarch (*Danaus plexippus*).

The Camberwell Beauty is a very rare migrant from Europe. There was an influx of Camberwell Beauty butterflies to the UK in 1995 and records in South West Scotland include sightings from Tighnabruich, Argyll, and from Culzean Country Park, Ayrshire. It was also seen in 1996 at Moine Mhor Nature Reserve, Kilmartin, Argyll. The record of the Monarch on 25th September 1999 on the island of Lismore, Argyll is thought to have originated from North America rather than an escape from a butterfly farm or breeder, as it coincided with observations of birds from America. The Brimstone was recorded near Dumfries and may have come from a wandering individual from Northern England. The Brimstone is unlikely to become established in South West Scotland due to the paucity of the caterpillar food plants, Alder Buckthorn and Common Buckthorn.

All three species of butterfly are of interest as records but due to their rarity as visitors to South West Scotland they do not represent any significance in terms of conservation status.

During the survey period no records were received of the Arran Brown (*Erebia ligea*), a butterfly found in many continental European countries and possibly recorded from South West Scotland in Argyll during the previous century (see Thomson, 1980 and Emmet & Heath 1990 for details of Scottish records).

Two butterflies have become recently extinct in South West Scotland, the Large Tortoiseshell and the Small Blue. The Large Tortoiseshell (*Nymphalis polychroros*) is generally regarded as an extinct butterfly in Britain. A few historic records, from the previous century, are known from Argyll, and from Dumfries & Galloway.

Small Blue *Cupido minimus*

The Small Blue has only recently become extinct in South West Scotland, with the last confirmed example being recorded at Rockcliffe, Dumfries & Galloway in 1980. The Small Blue was never common, but it was widespread and a list of confirmed records are presented in Table 1.

During the survey period (1995-2004) it was hoped that the Small Blue would be found. Sadly, no records were received. This is particularly disturbing as there is currently, plenty of apparently suitable habitat at coastal locations in Ayrshire and in Dumfries & Galloway. Suitable habitat comprises sheltered, warm locations where Kidney Vetch, the caterpillar food plant, is growing in grassland that is kept short by either grazing, management or erosion. In the absence of some sort of disturbance this habitat will quickly develop into rough grassland and even scrub. The ephemeral nature of the favoured habitat may quickly result in local extinctions. It is now feared that the Small Blue has been lost from South West Scotland. The Small Blue can however survive in small populations, occupying a relatively small area, and it is hoped that this publication will stimulate a further search for this diminutive butterfly.

(opposite) The Camberwell Beauty is a rare migrant from Europe. The individual on the right was photographed at Culzean Country Park, 1995

(above) Small Blue on Kidney Vetch, the caterpillar food plant.

Small Blue, a butterfly that has recently become extinct in South West Scotland

Small Blue 1995-2004

| Jan | Feb | Mar | Apr | May | Jun | Jul | Aug | Sep | Oct | Nov | Dec |

A phenogram of Small Blue records (1995-2004) found elsewhere in Scotland

Table 1: Summary of records of Small Blue in South West Scotland since 1900

Site	O.S Grid Reference	Year
Kilmory	NR92	1900
Arran, Whiting Bay	NS02	1900
Ardrossan	NS24	1900
Troon	NS33	1900
Dumbarton	NS47	1900
Monkton	NS32	1900
Govan	NS56	1900
Portpatrick	NW95	1929
Port William	NX34	1929, 1939
Corsemalzie, Mochrum	NX35	1929, 1939
Glen Mills	NX97	1929
Spedlings Castle	NY08	1929
Portpatrick	NX0054	1939
Lochanhead	NX97	1939
Castle Hill Point, Rockcliffe	NX85	1960
Prestwick	NS3427	1970
Rockcliffe	NX865526	1974
Rockcliffe	NX85	1980

Aberrant Behaviour
and Unusual Colour Variations

During the ten year survey period there were few reports of unusual behaviour shown by butterflies or strange colour variations in South West Scotland.

A notable exception was the observation at Balloch Castle Country Park, Dunbartonshire in July 2001 of a male Ringlet paired with a female Meadow Brown (K. Futter pers.obs.). A rare example of mistaken identity. A contributory factor could have been that in this particular instance only a few Meadow Browns were seen (15) of which most were female, but Ringlets were more numerous (80) of which most were males. This could have led to a shortage of same-species mates, resulting in the abnormal pairing. This abnormal pairing may also have arisen due to the fact that the Ringlet is experiencing an expansion in range in Dunbartonshire, and in 2001 the grasslands at Balloch Castle Country Park were at the frontier of the expansion. The stress of not finding a female Ringlet at the frontier may have been a contributory cause to the unusual pairing.

Mistaken identity. A male Ringlet (below) pairing with a female Meadow Brown (above)

A normal pairing. Note the pale eye colour of the female (above) compared with the dark brown eyes of the male (below)

Unusual courtship behaviour was also observed between a male Small Tortoiseshell and a female Pearl-bordered Fritillary at Laggan, Sandyhills, Dumfries & Galloway on 23rd April 2003 (R. Sutcliffe pers.obs.). The courtship did not however lead to a mating attempt. There was only one male Small Tortoiseshell at the site, and there were 11 Pearl-bordered Fritillaries, which were out unusually early in the year.

Small Tortoiseshell courting a Pearl-bordered Fritillary

Normal courtship behaviour

Interesting colour variations recorded included all yellow forms, of the aberration *flava,* of the Small White and the Green-veined White during the second brood in Dunbartonshire (K. Futter pers.obs). The intensity and uniformity of the yellow was such that superficially they resembled a Clouded Yellow when viewed at a distance. In 2005, outside the atlas recording period, a Meadow Brown in Dumbarton (NS393758) was observed with a white hindwing (K. Futter, 17th July 2005). A colour variation found elsewhere in Britain and in other species and is thought to be caused by a pathological condition (Emmet & Heath 1990).

The Scotch Argus has several colour forms (Emmet & Heath 1990). In South West Scotland both male and female Scotch Argus are variable in the colour of the underside hindwing.

Yellow-brown form of the female Scotch Argus

Dark brown form of the female Scotch Argus

Dark female with a grey-violet hindwing band above a pale brown form of the male

Dark male form with the grey-violet hindwing band

Common Blue females show a wide variety of blue coloration on the upper wing surfaces in South West Scotland. The blue form *mariscolore* is a particularly beautiful variation.

Female Common Blue, *mariscolore* form

Typical female Common Blue coloration

The Small Copper is another variable species. The blue spotted form *caeruleopunctata* is a common aberration. Other individuals are heavily suffused with a green sheen and some are pale in colour with the coppery orange appearing to be washed out.

Small Copper with blue spots on the hindwings, *caeruleopunctata* form

Small Copper with pale orange upper wings. This form is more common during the later broods of September

A particularly interesting colour variation is shown by the Dark Green Fritillary. The *scotica* subspecies is much darker than the normal colour form and both forms can be seen flying in the same colony.

A female Dark Green Fritillary *scotica* form (Ayrshire)

A normal coloured female Dark Green Fritillary

Trends

South West Scotland and a Comparison with Other Parts of the UK

An analysis of the results of the ten year survey between 1995-2004 allow us to make a judgement on which butterflies are doing well and which are not. A summary of the status of the main species is shown in Table 2.

When comparing the two five-year periods to determine changes in the distribution and abundance of butterflies, there is always the difficulty of bias associated with differences in recording effort. In the first five year period there was a great deal of enthusiasm in recording butterflies because it was part of a national scheme which led to the publication of the Millennium Atlas in 2001. Therefore it is likely that some sites may not have been re-visited during the second five year period which yielded positive sightings in the first five year period. Despite this caveat it is nonetheless possible to provide a relatively accurate assessment of trends from the local knowledge of observers and by examining the mapped data as a whole.

It was hoped that during the survey the Small Blue butterfly would be located but no confirmed records were received. Sadly, another butterfly that may follow the Small Blue into extinction is the Dingy Skipper. The results of our survey show that this Skipper has become a very rare butterfly. The colonies around Mabie Forest, Dalbeattie and Luce Bay, Dumfries & Galloway now appear to be the only remaining strongholds. The decline seen in our branch area is unfortunately mirrored in many other parts of Britain and Europe. It is unclear why this butterfly has decreased in numbers so rapidly as the larval food plant, Birdsfoot-trefoil is very common.

A Dingy Skipper from Mabie Forest, one of the few remaining sites of this declining butterfly

The Pearl-bordered Fritillary (top) and Small Pearl-bordered Fritillary (bottom) have British stronghold populations in South West Scotland

Local colonies of the Common Blue, Small Heath and Grayling have also disappeared as a consequence of development on urban waste ground and from changes in land management.

It is not all doom and gloom. The Pearl-bordered Fritillary and Small Pearl-bordered Fritillary currently have important populations in our branch area which appear to be relatively stable. This contrasts with other parts of Britain, where these fritillaries, particularly the Pearl-bordered Fritillary, have experienced rapid declines. The Pearl-bordered Fritillary sites require ongoing monitoring to ensure their stability as the populations in South West Scotland now represent important British strongholds. The Small Pearl-bordered Fritillary is fortunately widespread in South West Scotland and appears to have shown local expansions in its range recently, particularly in Dunbartonshire, due largely to recent management at forestry plantations that have created a patchwork of scrub, woodland and marshy flushes that the butterfly favours.

The Large Heath is another butterfly causing concern, with the disappearance of some colonies during the survey period. The problem with the Large Heath is that its preferred habitat of wet heathland and lowland raised bog is becoming increasingly fragmented and threatened by development and drainage.

Unfortunately, we still do not know enough about the status of the Marsh Fritillary as it is a very difficult species to monitor due to its fluctuating population size. A recent survey of known sites found a worrying number to be in poor condition (SNH unpublished data).

Some species have done well during the survey period and have increased in distribution and abundance. The Ringlet has shown an expansion in range in Dunbartonshire, Lanarkshire, North Ayrshire, Argyll and Glasgow since the early 1990s. The Orange-tip has shown a similar increase in range throughout Scotland since 1993/94 and continues to be widespread and relatively common.

The Peacock has shown a continuing expansion in range since 1996 and has colonised many new areas particularly in Greater Glasgow and Dunbartonshire, where it is now a widespread, resident breeding species. The increase in range shown by these species is almost certainly associated with climate change, in particular with a tendency for winters to be milder.

The Ringlet (left) and Orange-tip (right) have both increased in range during the survey

The Peacock has also increased its range. This female has a damaged right hindwing as a result of an unsuccessful bird attack. Birds are more likely to peck at false eye spots on the wing than the body

The emerging trend of the climate affecting the distribution of butterflies in South West Scotland seems to be supported by the remarkable establishment in our branch area during the survey period of the Comma. The Holly Blue is at its northern limit in Dumfries & Galloway but it also seems to have maintained a foothold along the Solway Coast in recent years.

The Holly Blue has now established a foothold in Dumfries & Galloway. Female underside

Female Holly Blue, second brood with a greater amount of black to the wing tips

The Comma has been recorded in several areas of South West Scotland. This individual was photographed in Lockerbie, Dumfries & Galloway

Other species in England are pushing northwards which have not yet reached South West Scotland. These include the Gatekeeper (*Pyronia tithonus*), the Small Skipper (*Thymelicus sylvestris*) and White-letter Hairstreak (*Satyrium w-album*). It is possible that in the near future these species may be added to the Lepidoptera fauna of South West Scotland.

For the species showing a decline or threatened elsewhere in Britain it is important that these species are targeted for recording in future years and trends monitored. The Marsh Fritillary in particular requires monitoring due to the cyclical fluctuations in numbers and the uncertain impact of parasitism. Although the parasitic wasps can decimate a population of caterpillars, one benefit of the parasite is that it keeps the population in check to avoid the caterpillars in a colony eating all the available foodplant (Barnett & Warren 1995).

The underside of a Marsh Fritillary showing the orange legs, palps and antennae undersides

Marsh Fritillary caterpillars are gregarious when immature

A parasitized Marsh Fritillary caterpillar. The caterpillar is already dead and has the cocoons of the parasitic wasp *Cotesia melitaearum* on it

A chrysalis of the Marsh Fritillary

Table 2: Status of butterflies found in South West Scotland

Family		Type	Status
Hesperidiae (Skippers)			
Chequered Skipper	*Carterocephalus palaemon*	Resident	local, stable
Large Skipper	*Ochlodes venata*	Resident	local, stable
Dingy Skipper	*Erynnis tages*	Resident	rare, declining
Pieridae (Whites)			
Clouded Yellow	*Colias croceus*	Immigrant	erratic
Large White	*Pieris brassicae*	Resident	widespread
Small White	*Pieris rapae*	Resident	widespread
Green-veined White	*Pieris napi*	Resident	common
Orange-tip	*Anthocharis cardamines*	Resident	widespread
Lycaenidae (Hairstreaks, Coppers and Blues)			
Green Hairstreak	*Callophrys rubi*	Resident	local, stable
Purple Hairstreak	*Neozephyrus quercus*	Resident	local, stable
Small Copper	*Lycaena phlaeas*	Resident	widespread
Northern Brown Argus	*Aricia artaxerxes*	Resident	local, stable
Common Blue	*Polyommatus icarus*	Resident	widespread
Holly Blue	*Celastrina argiolus*	Resident	very local
Nympahlidae (Vanessids, Fritillaries and Browns)			
Red Admiral	*Vanessa atalanta*	Immigrant	widespread
Painted Lady	*Vanessa cardui*	Immigrant	widespread
Small Tortoiseshell	*Aglais urticae*	Resident	widespread
Peacock	*Inachis io*	Resident	widespread and increasing
Comma	*Polygonia c-album*	Resident	recent coloniser
Small Pearl-bordered Fritillary	*Boloria selene*	Resident	widespread
Pearl-bordered Fritillary	*Boloria euphrosyne*	Resident	local, vulnerable
Dark Green Fritillary	*Argynnis aglaja*	Resident	recent decline
Marsh Fritillary	*Euphydryas aurinia*	Resident	local, declining
Speckled Wood	*Pararge aegeria*	Resident	local, stable
Wall Brown	*Lasiommata megera*	Resident	local, stable
Mountain Ringlet	*Erebia epiphron*	Resident	local, stable
Scotch Argus	*Erebia aethiops*	Resident	locally common
Grayling	*Hipparchia semele*	Resident	local
Meadow Brown	*Maniola jurtina*	Resident	common
Ringlet	*Aphantopus hyperantus*	Resident	local, increasing
Small Heath	*Coenonympha pamphilus*	Resident	widespread
Large Heath	*Coenonympha tullia*	Resident	local,declining

Peat Bogs Under Threat

One of the most threatened habitats in South West Scotland is the lowland peat bog. As a result of drainage and over-management of the countryside many peat bogs have been destroyed and the remaining raised bogs are becoming isolated and threatened. Many of the peat bogs surrounding the City of Glasgow have been damaged beyond the reinstatement of a typical bog community, having suffered from habitat succession, mostly through drainage and urban encroachment. Most sites are now occupied by Birch woodland and grassland with remnants of heath. In the wider countryside pristine peat bogs can still be found and these will host the Large Heath butterfly. The Green Hairstreak, Small Pearl-bordered Fritillary and Small Heath may also be found alongside the Large Heath.

Although campaigns to save peatlands have had some success in raising the profile of peat bogs, they continue to remain undervalued.

In Dumfries & Galloway, at Dalbeattie, the Aucheninnes Moss (NX8560) is under grave threat from a landfill development. In Dunbartonshire, on the fringe of Helensburgh, part of the Blackhill Mire (NS3083) has been destroyed by the development of the Blackhill Light Industrial Estate, and the remainder is threatened by a golf course extension by the Helensburgh Golf Club. Both the Aucheninnes Moss and Blackhill Mire support the Large Heath butterfly – but for how much longer?

Good habitat at Blackhill Mire, Helensburgh

Destruction of butterfly habitat at Blackhill Mire

Bog vegetation scraped away at Blackhill Mire

The destruction of part of the Blackhill Mire for development

The presence of the Large Heath butterfly is a good indicator of the quality of a peat bog habitat. This quality is reflected by the presence of other indicator species alongside the Large Heath. For example, the Bog Bush Cricket (*Metrioptera brachyptera*) and Sorrel Pygmy Moth (*Enteucha acetosae*) are also found at Auchennines Moss – their only known Scottish Site (Buglife site survey 2003). At Blackhill Mire a rich selection of typical peatland moths was found such as Light Knot Grass (*Acronicta menyanthidis scotica*), Emperor Moth (*Saturnia pavonia*) and *Glyphipterix haworthana* (Keith Bland site survey 20th May 1995), and Glaucous Shears (*Papestra biren*) and Clouded Buff (*Diacrisia sannio*) (K. Futter pers.obs.).

The mire also supports the largest local colony of Green Hairstreak (K. Futter site survey 9th May 1991, provided a count of 128 Green Hairstreaks). In addition to supporting a valuable fauna the flora is also rich. At Blackhill mire, a typical M19 *Calluna vulgaris – Eriophorum vaginatum* mire community occurs. At pockets of marsh a large colony of the locally uncommon Narrow Buckler Fern can be found. At both Auchennines Moss and Blackhill Mire the locally uncommon Whorled Caraway is present. It is a sad fact that despite the obvious quality of these two sites, they have both been damaged and suffered neglect to the extent that the Large Heath butterfly may be lost from both sites.

Large Heath at Blackhill Mire, Helensburgh (19th July 1997), a site under threat from the extension of a golf course

A protest by conservationists and members of the local community to save Aucheninnes Moss, Dalbeattie from becoming damaged by landfill

The Importance of Wild Flowers

Ragwort, Dandelion, Lesser Knapweed, Marsh Thistle, Creeping Thistle and Bramble

Large areas of South West Scotland are without habitation and comprise sheep and cattle grazed pasture, moorland and hill slopes, which have few flowers to satisfy the nectar requirements of butterflies. As a consequence of this many resident butterflies tend to be more common along the coastal fringe, where there are more wild flowers and where habitation with gardens provide further nectaring opportunities. As a result of the over-management of the countryside resulting in fewer flowers, the more common wild flowers which can tolerate a variety of conditions become vitally important for butterflies.

The Common Ragwort, a much maligned plant, is one of the most important nectar providing plants for butterflies in South West Scotland because of its long flowering period. It is especially favoured by the Small Copper and is used by many other species including the Large Skipper, Small Heath, Holly Blue, Common Blue and Grayling. The humble Dandelion, also regarded as a pernicious weed is a very important nectar plant for spring butterflies, including the Pearl-bordered Fritillary. Other important spring nectar sources include the Bugle, Pussy Willow and the blossom of Blackthorn.

The Lesser Knapweed is a very important flower in late summer when many other flowers have finished and it provides nectar for the Peacock, Meadow Brown, Large White, Small White, Green-veined White, Small Copper and the migratory Painted Lady and Red Admiral.

Holly Blue on Ragwort

Grayling on Ragwort

The Marsh Thistle is a crucial plant for the Small Pearl-bordered Fritillary as it is often the only suitable nectar plant in the wet grassland and flushes occupied by this species. The flowering time in mid summer means that Marsh Thistle is also important for the Chequered Skipper near the end of its flight time and for the Scotch Argus at the beginning of its flight time. There are other thistles of similar importance to butterflies particularly the Creeping Thistle, another despised weed, which is a clear favourite of the Small Tortoiseshell.

The Bramble loved for its fruit, but hated for its thorns and rambling habit is a key nectar provider for many butterflies at the edge of a wood or hedgerow and the flowers are frequently visited by species such as Ringlet, Meadow Brown, Scotch Argus, Large Skipper and Green-veined White.

The Ragwort, Dandelion, Bramble and Creeping Thistle are often considered to be weeds and destroyed without thought, but these common flowers are favoured by butterflies and they are as important as the caterpillar food plant for their survival and conservation.

Other important wild flowers that provide nectar include the Cuckoo Flower, Birdsfoot-trefoil, Heather, Cross-leaved Heath, Bell Heather, Bloody Cranesbill, Hemp Agrimony, Daisy, Devil's-bit Scabious, Common Cats-ear, Heath Spotted Orchid and Tormentil.

Small Tortoisehell on Creeping Thistle, a favourite nectar source in the wider countryside

The Importance of the Stinging Nettle

The Stinging Nettle or 'Jaggy' as it is known locally, is the foodplant of the caterpillar of many of our familiar garden butterflies. The Peacock, Small Tortoiseshell, Red Admiral, Comma and occasionally Painted Lady caterpillars all require the Stinging Nettle as a foodplant. Indeed, these butterflies constitute over fifteen percent of the butterfly species found in South West Scotland.

The widespread tidying of the countryside and the development of waste ground can often result in the destruction of patches of Stinging Nettle that were suitable as foodplants for butterfly caterpillars. The Peacock and Small Tortoiseshell need large patches of Stinging Nettle that receive the full sun. Clumps of nettles that are on fertile soil, or even growing next to a manure heap are often chosen in preference to stunted or non vigorous nettles. The Small Tortoiseshell and Peacock lay their eggs as a mass and the young caterpillars feed communally in a protective silk tent. When maturing the caterpillars disperse within the nettle patch to feed on their own. A large number of nettle plants are therefore required to sustain a colony of caterpillars. In a woodland setting nettles that are in the shade or beneath trees and shrubs are avoided. Patches of nettles in a garden are usually also avoided (Gaston *et al.* 2004).

The Red Admiral and Comma also require vigorous Stinging Nettle plants that receive full sun, but do not require clumps of nettles. The eggs are laid singly and the caterpillars are solitary and do not require large numbers of nettle plants.

Mature Small Tortoiseshell caterpillar

Mature Peacock caterpillar

A side view of a tent of leaves, the retreat of a Red Admiral caterpillar, partially visible on the right

Another view of the tent of leaves, with the caterpillar's head visible near the centre

Red Admiral chrysalis

Red Admiral fully formed inside the chrysalis

Mature Comma caterpillar on Stinging Nettle. Breeding was not confirmed in South West Scotland during the survey period

Butterfly	Caterpillar Foodplant	Favoured nectar sources
Chequered Skipper *Carterocephalus palaemon*	Purple Moor-grass	Bugle, Marsh Thistle, Bluebell, Tormentil, White Clover
Large Skipper *Ochlodes venata*	Cocksfoot, other grasses	Thistles, Bramble, Ragwort, Bloody Cranesbill
Dingy Skipper *Erynnis tages*	Birdsfoot-trefoil	Birdsfoot-trefoil
Clouded Yellow *Colias croceus*	Clovers	Clovers, Thistles, Hawkweeds, Sow-thistles, other composites
Large White *Pieris brassicae*	Cultivated Cabbage, Nasturtium, Sea Radish	Lesser Knapweed, Buddleia, Lavender, other garden flowers
Small White *Pieris rapae*	Cultivated Cabbage, Nasturtium, crucifers	Dandelion, Lesser Knapweed, crucifers, Creeping Thistle
Green-veined White *Pieris napi*	Garlic Mustard, Cuckoo Flower, crucifers	Cuckoo Flower, Bramble, Daisy, Lesser Knapweed, Bluebell, Red Clover, Thistles
Orange-tip *Anthocharis cardamines*	Garlic Mustard, Cuckoo Flower, Dame's Violet	Cuckoo Flower, Dame's Violet, Garlic Mustard, Bluebell, Honesty, Forget-Me-Nots
Green Hairstreak *Callophrys rubi*	Blaeberry, Gorse Birdsfoot-trefoil	Blaeberry, Bluebell, Birdsfoot-trefoil,
Purple Hairstreak *Neozephyrus quercus*	Oaks	Aphid honeydew on Oaks, Ash, Sycamore
Small Copper *Lycaena phlaeas*	Sorrel, Sheep's Sorrel, docks	Ragwort, Lesser Knapweed, Daisy, Bloody Cranesbill
Northern Brown Argus *Aricia artaxerxes*	Rock-rose	Rock-rose, Bloody Cranesbill, Thyme, Tufted Vetch
Common Blue *Polyommatus icarus*	Birdsfoot-trefoil, Greater Birdsfoot-trefoil	Birdsfoot-trefoil, Ragwort
Holly Blue *Celastrina argiolus*	Holly, Ivy	Aphid honeydew on trees, Ragwort, Bramble
Red Admiral *Vanessa atalanta*	Stinging Nettle	Thistles, Lesser Knapweed Buddleia, Michaelmas Daisy
Painted Lady *Vanessa cardui*	Thistles, Stinging Nettle	Buddleia, Creeping Thistle, many garden flowers
Small Tortoiseshell *Aglais urticae*	Stinging Nettle	Creeping Thistle, Ragwort, Lesser Knapweed, Buddleia, Hemp Agrimony
Peacock *Inachis io*	Stinging Nettle	Lesser Knapweed, Thistles, Hemp Agrimony, Buddleia
Comma *Polygonia c-album*	Stinging Nettle	Ivy Flowers, Thistles, Buddleia

Small Pearl-bordered Fritillary *Boloria selene*	Marsh Violet, Common Dog Violet	Marsh Thistle, Ragged Robin
Pearl-bordered Fritillary *Boloria euphrosyne*	Common Dog Violet, Marsh Violet	Bugle, Birdsfoot-trefoil, Bluebell, Dandelion
Dark Green Fritillary *Argynnis aglaja*	Common Dog Violet, Marsh Violet	Lesser Knapweed, Bramble, Spear & Creeping Thistles
Marsh Fritillary *Euphydryas aurinia*	Devil's-bit Scabious	Thistles
Speckled Wood *Pararge aegeria*	Cock's-foot, Couch, Yorkshire Fog, grasses	Aphid honeydew on Ash, Oak Birch, Alder; Bramble
Wall Brown *Lasiommata megera*	Cock's-foot, Fescues, Yorkshire Fog, Bents	Ragwort, Bramble, composites
Mountain Ringlet *Erebia epiphron*	Mat-grass, Sheep's Fescue	Tormentil, upland flowers
Scotch Argus *Erebia aethiops*	Purple Moor-grass, other grasses	Marsh Thistle, Devil's-bit Scabious, Heath Spotted Orchid, Heather
Grayling *Hipparchia semele*	Fescues, Bents, other grasses	Ragwort, Buddleia, Bramble
Meadow Brown *Maniola jurtina*	Fescues, Bents, Meadow grasses	Bramble, Lesser Knapweed, Ragwort
Ringlet *Aphantopus hyperantus*	Cock's-foot, other grasses	Bramble, Rosebay Willowherb, Creeping Buttercup, Cat's Ear
Small Heath *Coenonympha pamphilus*	Red Fescue, Bents, Sheep's Fescue	Ragwort, Heather, Tormentil
Large Heath *Coenonympha tullia*	Hare's-tail Cotton-grass	Cross-leaved Heath, Bell Heather

Northern Brown Argus nectaring on Tufted Vetch

The Importance of Garden Flowers

In addition to wild flowers, there are many garden flowers that provide rich nectar sources for butterflies in South West Scotland. The wet and cooler climate may however result in fewer flowering plants available to butterflies when compared to southern England. For example, the Incense Bush (*Eupatorium ligustrinum*) is a plant that can swarm with butterflies in August in southern England but struggles to flower in Dunbartonshire by mid September. The butterflies that are attracted to garden plants are predominantly the migratory species that require a nectar rich diet to fuel their frenetic flight activity.

The Butterfly Bush or Buddleia (*Buddleia davidii*) is a clear favourite as a nectar source in many gardens. At some waste ground sites in Glasgow during the 1990s there were large patches of Buddleia, but many of these sites have now been developed or are in the process of being developed, particularly along the margins of the River Clyde. At the waste ground sites along the Clyde Walkway between Dalmarnock and Carmyle it was possible to see the odd sight of the Grayling nectaring on Buddleia, but the Grayling has diminished in numbers in recent years in Glasgow.

The Orange-tip can be a regular visitor to gardens particularly if the caterpillar foodplants are present

Carefully chosen varieties and species of Buddleia can extend the flowering season from late May to early November. The Orange Ball Butterfly Bush (*Buddleia globosa*) is in bloom from late May to late June. They are favoured by moths but will also attract butterflies. The familiar Buddleia is in flower from late June to the end of August and is a favourite of the Small Tortoiseshell, Peacock, Red Admiral, Painted Lady, Large White and Small White. The Orange Ball Butterfly Bush x Buddleia hybrid (*globosa* x *davidii*), known as the Hybrid Butterfly Bush (*Buddleia x weyeriana*) is in flower from mid August to early November. The Hybrid Butterfly Bush is especially good at attracting the Red Admiral, Painted Lady and Large White in September and October.

During May and early June when the Orange-tips are flying, the garden flowers of Honesty, Perennial Honesty, Dame's Violet, Aubretia and Forget-me-nots will often be used as nectar sources together with Cuckoo Flower and Garlic Mustard that may also be present in some gardens. The Green-veined White and Small White may nectar on the Dandelion and Daisy plants in a flowering lawn.

The summer months of July and August typically see gardens looking their best with many flowers competing for the attention of pollinating insects. Valuable garden plants for butterflies that can tolerate the climate of South West Scotland include Purpletop Verbena (*Verbena bonariensis*), Lavenders, Marjoram, Mints, Erigeron and Felicia daisies, Lobelia species, simple flowered Dahlias and Asters. With the onset of autumn, the varieties of Michaelmas Daisy and Ice Plant 'Autumn Joy' (*Sedum spectabile*) are particularly good at attracting butterflies, most notably the Red Admiral.

The more flowers a garden has the more likely it will attract butterflies. Many of the National Trust gardens, such as Greenbank Gardens, Glasgow; Culzean Country Park, Ayrshire, and Threave Gardens, Castle Douglas are good places to see Red Admiral, Small Tortoiseshell, Painted Lady, Large White and the Peacock.

In addition to flowers, the gardens that have fruit trees will also attract butterflies as they feed on the juices of over ripe fruit that has fallen to the ground.

Female Red Admiral on a fallen plum

The Red Admiral (left) and the Painted Lady (right) are migrants that favour garden flowers as nectaring sources

Butterflies of South West Scotland

T his section of the book highlights some of the sites at which you can see the butterflies featured in the species section. They have been chosen for their ease of access. Many of the sites are Scottish Wildlife Trust reserves and other nature reserves or protected areas.

A summary of the butterfly interest of each region is provided together with a selection of sites that can normally reward visitors with a view of the target species. It should always be borne in mind that the climate of South West Scotland is not always favourable for butterfly watching! An examination of the weather forecast is a wise option before embarking on a long journey to a particular site, for example to see the Chequered Skipper in Argyll or the Mountain Ringlet at Ben Lawers or Ben Lui.

A mating pair of Chequered Skippers, the female is above the male

Dumfries & Galloway
(Vice Counties 72, 73 and 74)

DUMFRIES & Galloway remains a tranquil and largely overlooked corner of Scotland. It claims a diversity of wildlife and habitats few regions can match, from its mountain and moorland, woodland and farmland, peatland and grassland down to the rich sheltered shores of the Solway Firth. It has a unique and rich biodiversity due largely to its mild climate influenced by the warm Gulf Stream and a long coastline with a predominantly southerly aspect. Its diversity reflects its position as an area supporting species both at their northern limits such as the Holly Blue and those at their southern limits such as the Scotch Argus. It is one of the best regions in Scotland for migrant butterflies such as Painted Lady and Clouded Yellow. Indeed 29 species of butterfly were recorded in Dumfries & Galloway during the survey, making it the richest region for butterflies in South West Scotland.

Dumfries & Galloway supports important populations of Pearl-bordered Fritillary, Northern Brown Argus, Large Heath and Scotch Argus. There is some concern that Dingy Skipper may be in serious decline as may be the Dark Green Fritillary. One species now apparently extinct to the region is the Small Blue. However this region is also the first to record species expanding their range from the south such as the Comma.

Much of Dumfries & Galloway has undergone a dramatic transformation in the last half century. Afforestation claimed large areas of heathland and moorland. Agricultural intensification of farmland has led to losses of herb-rich grassland and wet meadows; more sheep and fewer cattle has led to changes in grazing; while a reduction in traditional management of native woodland and Bracken has resulted in some loss of sheltered open habitats so valuable to butterfly populations. Other threats include loss of valuable lowland raised bogs to afforestation, peat cutting, golf courses and to landfill. Such losses continue today with the imminent loss of Aucheninnes Moss, an important site for Large Heath and Small Pearl-bordered Fritillary, to landfill extension.

A Pearl-bordered Fritillary, one of the butterfly highlights of Dumfries & Galloway

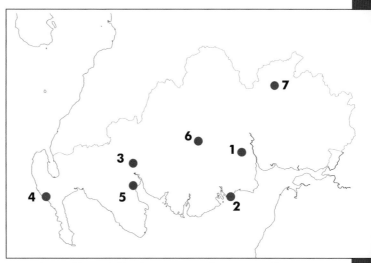

Location of butterfly sites in Dumfries & Galloway

1. Lochaber Loch Forest Nature Reserve, Mabie Forest

2. Rockcliffe to Port o' Warren Coast (to Portling)

3. Cree Valley Woodlands – Knockman Wood, Wood of Cree, Camer woods, Glen Trool

The Isle of Whithorn (NX4836) on the Solway coast. The Solway Coast is home to many butterflies including the Northern Brown Argus and Wall Brown

4. Portpatrick, Port Kale, Southern Upland Way, Dunskey Estate and Mull of Galloway

5. Carsegowan Moss Scottish Wildlife Trust Reserve

6. Knowetop Lochs Scottish Wildlife Trust Reserve

7. Earshaig to Mosshope on the Southern Upland Way

Dumfries and Galloway butterfly sites

1. Lochaber Loch Forest Nature Reserve, Mabie Forest
(NX9270). OS Landranger 84, Explorer 313

Plantation, ancient woodland and scrub from Mabie House west to Lochaber Loch. This site is managed for its butterfly interest by the Forestry Commission. There is an extensive network of footpaths and cycle tracks.

Target Species: Pearl-bordered Fritillary, and Small Pearl-bordered Fritillary

Other Species: Large Skipper, Dingy Skipper, Green-veined White, Orange-tip, Green Hairstreak, Purple Hairstreak, Small Copper, Common Blue, Peacock, Dark Green Fritillary, Wall Brown, Meadow Brown, Ringlet and Small Heath.

Parking: Car park, toilets and picnic area are located at Mabie Forest off the A710 south west of Dumfries (NX950710). Cycle hire is also available.

Mabie Forest near Dumfries

Castlehill Point, Rockcliffe

2. Rockcliffe to Port o' Warren Coast (to Portling)
(NX850535 to NX880535).
OS Landranger 84, Explorer 313

This coastal walk from Rockcliffe follows a National Trust for Scotland route to Castlehill Point. An exceptionally scenic footpath then follows the coast east to Port o' Warren.

Target Species: Northern Brown Argus, Grayling, Dingy Skipper, Holly Blue, Large Skipper, Wall Brown, and Small Pearl-bordered Fritillary.

Other Species: Green-veined White, Common Blue, Small Tortoiseshell, Meadow Brown, Small Heath and Ringlet. Also Forester Moth (*Adscita statices*), Cinnabar (*Tyria jacobaeae*) and Six-spot Burnet Moth (*Zygaena filipendulae*).

Parking: Car Park off the Colvend to Rockcliffe road at NX851535.

3. Cree Valley Woodlands – Knockman Wood, Wood of Cree, Camer woods, Glen Trool
OS Landranger 77, Explorer 319

Target Species: Purple Hairstreak, Scotch Argus and Dark Green Fritillary.

Other Species: Small Pearl-bordered Fritillary, Large Skipper, Orange-tip, Small Copper, Small Heath, Ringlet and Meadow Brown.

Parking: Car Parks at Knockman Wood (NX408674), Wood of Cree (NX380709), High Camer Wood (NX366732), Caldons (NX396790) and Loch Trool (for Glen Trool, Buchan and Glenhead woods) (NX415804).

Wood of Cree

4. Portpatrick, Port Kale, Southern Upland Way, Dunskey Estate and Mull of Galloway
OS Landranger 82, Explorer 309

Coastal habitats

Target Species: Wall Brown, Grayling, Large Skipper, Dingy Skipper, Northern Brown Argus.

Other Species: Meadow Brown and Small Heath.

Parking: Car Parks at Portpatrick (NX000537), Port Logan (NX096411) and Mull of Galloway (NX155305).

Mull of Galloway, left, Portpatrick right

Dumfries & Galloway

5. Carsegowan Moss Scottish Wildlife Trust Reserve

(NX422592). OS Landranger 83, Explorer 311

Lowland raised bog. The Scottish Wildlife Trust are restoring this site by raising the water table and clearing the trees.

Target species: Large Heath.

Other species: Green-veined White, Orange-tip, Small Copper, Peacock and Red Admiral.

Parking: SWT car park at NX422594 off the A714.

Carsegowan Moss Scottish Wildlife Trust Reserve

6. Knowetop Lochs Scottish Wildlife Trust Reserve

(NX7078). OS Landranger 84, Explorer 320

Heathland

Target Species: Large Heath and Scotch Argus.

Other Species: Green-veined White, Orange-tip, Small Copper, Small Pearl-bordered Fritillary, Red Admiral, Painted Lady, Small Tortoiseshell, Peacock, Meadow Brown, Small Heath and Ringlet. Day flying moths include Northern Eggar (*Lasiocampa quercus*), Clouded Buff (*Diacrisia sannio*) and Red Necked Footman (*Atolmis rubricollis*).

Parking: Car park beside the A712 at NX706788.

7. Earshaig to Mosshope on the Southern Upland Way

OS Landranger 78, Explorer 330/322
This is a long walk through conifer plantation but the ride is extra wide due to the gas pipeline.

Target species: Scotch Argus, Small Pearl-bordered Fritillary and Dark Green Fritillary.

Other species: Large Skipper and Common Blue.

Parking: Car park at Earshaig (NT050024), on the road west of Beattock.

Knowetop Lochs Scottish Wildlife Trust Reserve

Butterflies of South West Scotland

Ayrshire
(Vice County 75)

ALTHOUGH there are 26 species of butterfly regularly recorded in Ayrshire, a relatively low number compared to southern England, Ayrshire is nonetheless a very important vice county for butterflies at a local and national level. The populations of Northern Brown Argus, Small Pearl-bordered Fritillary, Large Heath and Scotch Argus are particularly significant. The Wall Brown has shown a recent decline in England but Ayrshire colonies have bucked the trend and are stable and doing well. The Grayling, another species that has shown some declines in Britain is also widespread along the Ayrshire coast but has experienced a local reduction in numbers between Troon and Irvine. Although many species of butterfly in Ayrshire are relatively stable, the population of Dingy Skipper has shown a dramatic fall and may be on the verge of extinction. The Dark Green Fritillary population has also experienced some worrying local declines.

The geology in Ayrshire is complex, but dominated by old red sandstone and Carboniferous volcanic rocks, and at a few local sites some areas of base-rich rocks. The base-rich rocks are important for butterflies as they support the herb-rich grassland habitats favoured by many butterflies. The best sites have Common Rock-rose and Bloody Cranesbill and these often host strong colonies of the Northern Brown Argus.

A mating pair of Northern Brown Arg
Several colonies of t
butterfly can be four
Ayrshire. The female
on the right

The landscape reflects the geology and Ayrshire has a mostly lowland character as a result of lying on the Midland Valley between the Highland Boundary Fault to the north and the Southern Upland Fault to the south. Dramatic scenery is however provided by the volcanic plug of Loudoun Hill and the microgranite of Ailsa Craig, and by the mountainous terrain beside Loch Doon. As a result of the landscape, large areas of Ayrshire are agricultural, with sheep and cattle grazing being widespread on the relatively gently sloping ground. Central Ayrshire also accommodates mixed farmland. The agricultural areas and some pockets of afforestation are largely unsuitable for butterflies, which are most abundant along the coast and at woodlands containing predominantly native trees.

The Ayrshire coast comprises many sandy beaches and dune systems and when sheltered from the wind and south facing these sites can be oases for butterflies such as Common Blue, Small Copper, Grayling, Dark Green Fritillary and Wall Brown. Areas of waste ground around derelict sites of industry, such as those at Stevenston are also occupied by many butterflies particularly the Common Blue and Grayling.

Away from the coast there are some isolated habitats that are particularly important for butterflies such as the raised bog at Dalmellington that supports the Large Heath and the herb-rich grassland at Feoch Meadow which supports the Scotch Argus. The Scotch Argus is also found on the old military road north from Loch Tulla across the Black Mount. The better woodlands host Purple Hairstreak, Small Pearl-bordered Fritillary, Large Skipper and Ringlet.

A roosting Common Blue in the typical head down posture. The Common Blue can be seen at many coastal sites in Ayrshire

Location of butterfly sites in Ayrshire

1. Feoch Meadows

2. Dalmellington Moss

3. Gailes Marsh

4. Knockentiber Disused Railway line

5. Bennane Lea

6. Changue Forest

7. Shallochwreck Burn, Currarie Port

A view of the coast along the A77 near Kennedy's Pass with Ailsa Craig in the background. This stretch of coast is a rich area for butterflies

Ayrshire butterfly sites

1. Feoch Meadows
(NX263822). OS Landranger 76, Explorer 317

Scottish Wildlife Trust Reserve 2 miles east of Barrhill on the A714, and at the end of a rough track. Herb-rich meadow and peatland.

Target Species: Scotch Argus, Large Skipper and Small Pearl-bordered Fritillary.

Other Species: Ringlet, Common Blue, Small Copper, Whites and Large Heath.

Parking: Park in the Reserve car park at NX263815.

Feoch Meadows Scottish Wildlife Trust Reserve

2. Dalmellington Moss
(NS465063). OS Landranger 77, Explorer 327

Scottish Wildlife Trust Reserve on the A713 north-west of Dalmellington. Lowland raised peat bog. Caution – care is required when visiting any bog due to hidden water channels in peat.

Target Species: Large Heath.

Other Species: Small Heath and Green-veined White.

Parking: Park at the entrance to the Chalmerston open cast site near Dalmellington (NS467065).

Dalmellington Moss Scottish Wildlife Trust Reserve

3. Gailes Marsh

(NS324358). OS Landranger 70, Explorer 333

Scottish Wildlife Trust Reserve near Irvine. A herb-rich grassland sheltered by a coniferous plantation. Pond surrounded by rush and sedges.

Target Species: Common Blue and occasional Dark Green Fritillary.

Other Species: Meadow Brown, Green-veined White, Large White, Small Heath. Large number of Cinnabar and Six-spot Burnet moths.

Parking: Park along a track off Marine Drive near the reserve entrance gate at NS323360.

Gailes Marsh Scottish Wildlife Trust Reserve

4. Knockentiber Disused Railway line

(NS393398). OS Landranger 70, Explorer 333

Sheltered railway cutting.

Target Species: Grayling and Ringlet.

Other Species: Common Blue, Small Copper and Small Tortoiseshell.

Parking: Park on the road at NS399395 or NS387399

Knockentiber disused railway line

Ayrshire

5. Bennane Lea

(NX091862). OS Landranger 76, Explorer 317

Steep coastal path, requiring care. Undercliff, roadside verge and coastal grassland.

Target Species: Northern Brown Argus, Large Skipper, Dark Green Fritillary and Wall Brown.

Parking: On old A77 at NX092859.

6. Changue Forest

(NX301925). OS Landranger 76, Explorer 317

Mixed woodland.

Target Species: Scotch Argus, Green Hairstreak, Orange-tip, Large Skipper, Ringlet.

Parking: From Barr Village drive east to Craigmalloch. Park car at NX287942. Follow forest walk signposted, 'Kirsty's Trail' to NX305924.

7. Shallochwreck Burn, Currarie Port

(NX061777, NX057780)
OS Landranger 76, Explorer 317

Herb-rich grassland on basic rocks and gully with oaks.

Target Species: Northern Brown Argus, Wall Brown, Grayling, Large Skipper and Dark Green Fritillary.

Other species: Ringlet, Purple Hairstreak at NX061777.

Parking: Park at the side of a farm track at NX 063770.

Mating pair of Wall Brown.
The female is on the left

Greater Glasgow
(Vice Counties 76, 77)

FOR the purposes of this book 'Greater Glasgow' covers a large area of South West Scotland and includes the urban City of Glasgow, East Dunbartonshire, East Renfrewshire, Renfrewshire and Inverclyde, North and South Lanarkshire. Despite Glasgow being the largest urban area in Scotland and containing about a fifth of the population there are many areas of greenspace, parks and gardens and it lives up to the origin of the name Glasgow – dear green place. The River Clyde and the Forth and Clyde Canal provide two important wildlife corridors.

There are many varied habitats in Greater Glasgow that include the ancient woodlands of the Clyde & Avon river valleys in South Lanarkshire, peatlands and moorland such as the Clyde Muirshiel Country Park in Inverclyde, wetlands and lochs, grasslands and urban waste ground.

Within the City, areas of waste ground can be a temporary haven for many butterflies such as Small Copper, Common Blue, Peacock, Small Tortoiseshell and migratory species. The Grayling has also been recorded, but the very nature of urban brownfield sites means they can be developed and built upon. In addition, scrub can take over, resulting in waste ground being suitable for butterflies for only a relatively short time period. The importance of wildlife corridors, such as the River Clyde means that butterflies can transfer from one patch of open waste ground to another.

Some valuable habitats for wildlife have become isolated in Glasgow due to land development. It is still possible to see the Small Pearl-bordered Fritillary, but numbers have declined recently and management may be required to ensure their survival. Garscadden Wood is also relatively isolated but supports a healthy population of Purple Hairstreak. Some of the area's peatlands have been drained or have been invaded by Birch and have lost their butterfly communities. The Green Hairstreak has survived but the Large Heath has fared less well.

Small Pearl-bordered Fritillary, one of the wildlife highlights in the City of Glasgow

Some butterflies have increased their range recently, possibly in response to changes in climate. The Orange-tip was the first butterfly to make a rapid expansion in range and is now a relatively common sight in Greater Glasgow. The Ringlet experienced a sudden expansion in range in the early 1990s in the Clyde and Avon river valleys from the south and from Dunbartonshire in the north with the result that the Ringlet is now found at many sites around Glasgow. The Peacock has made a similar expansive journey and is now a much more widespread species than it was ten years ago.

The Grayling has colonised some areas of urban waste ground in the City of Glasgow

Location of butterfly sites in Greater Glasgow

1. Garscadden Wood

2. Glen Moss

3. Cathkin Braes Country Park

4. Cornalees Bridge, Clyde Muirshiel Regional Park

5. Clyde Valley Woodlands – Hamilton High Parks, Lower Nethan Gorge, Falls of Clyde

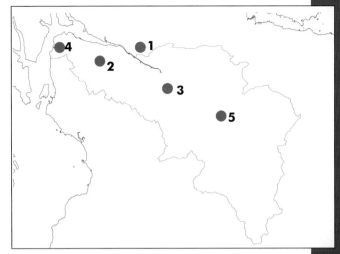

Meadow Brown.
A relatively common butterfly in
Greater Glasgow

Greater Glasgow butterfly sites

1. Garscadden Wood
(NS529720). OS Landranger 64, Explorer 342

Mature broad-leaved woodland on the border of vice county 77. One of the best places to see Purple Hairstreak, although binoculars may be needed to search the canopy.

Target species: Purple Hairstreak.

Other species: Large White, Small White, Green-veined White, Orange-tip, Small Tortoiseshell and Meadow Brown.

Parking: Park on Chesters Road, (off Station Road) at NS534717. Footpath leads into wood.

Garscadden Wood –
a very good site to see
Purple Hairstreak

Newly emerged Purple Hairstreaks

Butterflies of South West Scotland

2. Glen Moss

(NS368699). OS Landranger Number 63, Explorer 341

A Scottish Wildlife Trust Reserve. Peatland with open water

Target species: Small Pearl-bordered Fritillary.

Other Species: Green-veined White, Green Hairstreak, Meadow Brown and Ringlet

Parking: Park on the verge of the Kilmacolm to Houston minor road. Walk along the public footpath across the golf course to reach the reserve.

Glen Moss Scottish Wildlife Trust Reserve

3. Cathkin Braes Country Park

(NS6158). OS Landranger 64, Explorer 348.

Woodland, meadows and heathland.

Target Species: Small Pearl-bordered Fritillary, although there has been a recent, grave reduction in numbers.

Other Species: Green-veined White, Orange-tip, Small Copper, Small Tortoiseshell, Peacock, Ringlet and Meadow Brown.

Parking: Park on the Ardencraig road, in lay-byes along the Cathkin Road B759 or at the Viewpoint on Cathkin Road at NS618586.

4. Cornalees Bridge, Clyde Muirshiel Regional Park

(NS246721).
OS Landranger 63, Explorer 341.

Heathland, grassland and wooded glen

Target Species: Green Hairstreak and Small Pearl-bordered Fritillary.

Other species: Green-veined White, Small Copper, Small Tortoiseshell and Small Heath.

Parking: Car park and visitor centre with toilets.

5. Clyde Valley Woodlands – Hamilton High Parks, Lower Nethan Gorge, Falls of Clyde

OS Landranger 64, 71, 72, Explorer 335, 343

Ancient semi-natural woodland, herb-rich meadows and, at the Falls of Clyde, some stunning waterfalls and landscapes. Nethan Gorge and Falls of Clyde are Scottish Wildlife Trust reserves.

Target Species: Ringlet and Orange-tip.

Other Species: Green-veined White, Small White, Peacock and Small Tortoiseshell.

Parking: Hamilton High Parks (parking and visitor facilities at the Chatelherault Country Park NS736539); Lower Nethan Gorge (park at Crossford NS824471 to access the northern section via a footpath from the bridge on the Lanark road, the southern section can be accessed from Corramill Road at NS817459. Falls of Clyde is a major visitor attraction with a visitor centre (NS882425) and a large car park, follow signs for New Lanark World Heritage Site.

6. Walks along the Forth & Clyde Canal and Clyde Walkways

The path network beside the River Clyde and Forth & Clyde Canal is well maintained and passes through the City for several miles.

Species commonly seen include Green-veined White, Orange-tip, Small Copper, Small Tortoiseshell, Red Admiral, Painted Lady and Meadow Brown. The section of the Clyde Walkway beside the site of the former Dalmarnock Power Station, to Carmyle supported large numbers of Grayling in the 1990s and individuals may be seen in the general area.

The underside of a Small Tortoiseshell. This butterfly is often more common in gardens and urban areas than the wider countryside.

Dunbartonshire
(Vice County 99)

THE COUNTY of Dunbartonshire, together with Loch Lomond and its surrounds contain stunning scenery with varied and valuable habitats for butterflies and other wildlife. The beauty of the landscape centred around Loch Lomond was recognised by the creation of the first National Park in Scotland. The Loch Lomond and Trossochs National Park was inaugurated in July 2002 and includes a large area of Dunbartonshire.

To the south-west of the National Park lies the Firth of Clyde which is another important wildlife and landscape feature. In addition to supporting bird life of national importance the firth also hosts many tourist activities and the major Ministry of Defence submarine base at Faslane.

The generally wet and cool climate does not favour an abundance of butterflies, however 20 species have been recorded during the survey period. The most widespread species and the only butterfly that can be regarded as common is the Green-veined White. It can be found in large numbers in the lowland areas and is often the only butterfly encountered on hillsides.

Important populations of butterflies, at a national level, are found in the region and these comprise colonies of Scotch Argus, Small Pearl-bordered Fritillary and Large Heath. The Scotch Argus is locally common north of the Highland Boundary Fault and the Small Pearl-bordered Fritillary is widespread. Neither species seems to be declining but remain stable in numbers. The Large Heath occurs in smaller numbers at the few remaining bog and wet heathland habitats that have avoided agriculture, but all colonies remain vulnerable.

Green-veined White, a common butterfly in Dunbartonshire

The coastal fringe along the Firth of Clyde is the best location to find the summer migrants, Red Admiral, Painted Lady and the more erratic Clouded Yellow. The Small White and Large White are also more commonly found in the lowland areas near habitation and near to the firth. The Common Blue and Small Copper are local and also most commonly encountered close to the Clyde shore. The Common Blue has declined in recent years due to housing and utility developments on waste ground that previously hosted the butterfly.

A butterfly that is doing well in the region is the Green Hairstreak. Several populations are scattered throughout Dunbartonshire on wet heathland where it is possible to count over 100 individuals on a visit to some sites. Many of the peatland sites are vulnerable and a large colony at Blackhill Mire is unfortunately threatened by the proposed development of the Helensburgh Golf Course.

Green Hairstreak perched on Heather.
Large colonies of this beautiful butterfly can be found in Dunbartonshire

The Purple Hairstreak is found in Oak woodlands surrounding Helensburgh and Loch Lomondside, particularly at Glen Luss but they are difficult butterflies to spot high in the canopy.

The Small Heath normally found in small numbers can be found in greater numbers on the upland grasslands near Helensburgh and on some hill and mountain slopes.

Recent trends have shown an expansion in the range of some species, in particular the Orange-tip but also the Peacock and Ringlet. The Ringlet made a particularly significant push in range expansion in 2004 and 2005 with dispersal from its core site at Balloch Castle Country Park to the Clyde foreshore at the Brucehill Cliffs grassland, Dumbarton. The improving fortunes of the Ringlet and Peacock are almost certainly linked to climate warming, in particular the lack of severe winters.

Ringlet on Bramble, a favoured nectar source. This individual from Balloch Castle Country Park illustrates the grey hue found in many Ringlets from South West Scotland

Ringlet on Rosebay Willowherb at Balloch Castle Country Park. This individual has small rings of the aberration *parvipunctata*

Dunbartonshire

Location of butterfly sites in Dunbartonshire

1. Balloch Castle Country Park grassland

2. Brucehill Cliff grassland

3. Carman Muir, Renton

4. Helensburgh Upland Walkway

5. The Saltings Ecology Park, Old Kilpatrick, at foot of Erskine Bridge

6. Glen Douglas

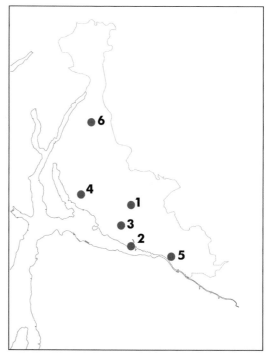

The Small Heath is a widespread butterfly in Dunbartonshire

Butterflies of South West Scotland

Dunbartonshire butterfly sites

1. Balloch Castle Country Park grassland

(NS388834). OS Landranger 56, Explorer 347

Flower-rich grassland meadows with Greater Butterfly Orchid.

Target Species: Ringlet.

Other species: Orange-tip, Meadow Brown, Green-veined White and the occasional Small Pearl-bordered Fritillary. Abundant Chimney Sweeper Moth (*Odezia atrata*).

Parking: Good parking and toilet facilities at the visitor centre.

Balloch Castle Country Park

2. Brucehill Cliff grassland

(NS384751). OS Landranger 63, Explorer 341

Flower-rich grassland beside an inland sandstone cliff. Royal Fern on the cliff face.

Target Species: Orange-tip during May and Peacock during August.

Other species: Green-veined White, Small Copper, Small Tortoiseshell, Meadow Brown.

Parking: Car Park at NS380753 or along the Clyde Shore Road adjacent to Levengrove Park at NS391748.

Brucehill Cliff grassland

3. Carman Muir, Renton

(NS367785) and surrounding moorland. OS Landranger 63, Explorer 347

Open heathland

Target Species: Green Hairstreak

Other Species: Green-veined White, Peacock, Small Pearl-bordered Fritillary and Small Heath.

Parking: Park along the Cardross Road beside the Carman Reservoir at NS376788.

Carman Muir

4. Helensburgh Upland Walkway

(NS298841 to NS283845).
OS Landranger 56, Explorer 347

Scenic walk through open woodland, grassland and forestry plantation.

Target Species: Small Pearl-bordered Fritillary.

Other Species: Green-veined White and Green Hairstreak.

Parking: Small Car park adjoining the Charles Rennie Mackintosh Hill House car park at NS301838. Well maintained footpath makes this an easy site to see Small Pearl-bordered Fritillaries.

Small Pearl-bordered Fritillary, a butterfly that is locally common in Dunbartonshire

5. The Saltings Ecology Park, Old Kilpatrick, at foot of Erskine Bridge

(NS464727) and the Forth & Clyde Canal, Bowling. OS Landranger 342, Explorer 64

Canal edged with trees and a circular walk around grassland at the Saltings. The Saltings support a flower-rich grassland. The tarmac footpath is suitable for disabled access.

Target Species: Orange-tip, Meadow Brown, Common Blue and Small Heath.

Parking: Park beside the canal on Dumbarton Road at NS466725 or on the Erskine Ferry Road at NS465725.

The Saltings, underneath the Erskine Bridge

6. Glen Douglas

(NS312986). OS Landranger 56, Explorer 364

Narrow through road alongside Douglas Water. Parts of the hill sides are fenced with no access due to Ministry of Defence land.

Target Species: Scotch Argus, in August is locally common in grassland with Bog Myrtle, beside the road

Other species: Green-veined White, Small Tortoiseshell, Peacock and Meadow Brown.

Parking: Limited to the roadside, although a good spot is NS268998.

Glen Douglas

Stirlingshire
(Vice County 86)

STIRLINGSHIRE covers a large area of the South West Scotland branch but with 22 species of butterfly recorded, it is not as rich in butterfly species as other areas. Nonetheless it has its specialities most notably the Mountain Ringlet and Large Heath. The extensive Oak woodland, particularly beside the eastern shore of Loch Lomond, also supports the largest number of Purple Hairstreaks in South West Scotland. There are also particularly important bog habitats in Stirlingshire with Flanders Moss being the largest area of intact lowland raised bog left in Britain. These bog sites provide a refuge for the Large Heath.

The Loch Lomond and Trossachs National Park recognises the environmental value of this whole area. Although there are extensive woodlands and upland hills there is also a broad flat valley plain that is cut by the River Forth. This comprises fertile silts and is dominated by a rich agricultural landscape.

The Mountain Ringlet occurs on Ben Lomond within Stirlingshire and at the Breadalbane range. The National Trust for Scotland Ben Lawers National Nature Reserve (NN609379) is in Perthshire and just beyond the boundary of the South West Scotland branch. It is mentioned here as it is one of the most accessible sites to see the Mountain Ringlet. The road to the Reserve is a well-maintained tarmac road off the A827 east of Killin. There is a visitor centre with a large carpark. The Mountain Ringlet can be found within the enclosed area of the Reserve and on the open hillsides.

A male Mountain Ringlet nectaring on Valerian at the Ben Lawers Nature Reserve

Stirlingshire

Location of butterfly sites in Stirlingshire

1. Wester Moss and Polmaise Bing, Fallin

2. Flanders Moss NNR

3. Mugdock Country Park

4. Loch Ardinning

5. Palacerigg Country Park, Cumbernauld

6. Burnside Wood, Kippen

7. Cashel

8. Sallochy

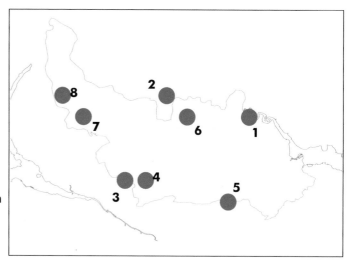

Ben Lomond and Loch Lomond. The Mountain Ringlet survives the frost and snow on Ben Lomond, its most southerly site in Scotland

Sites to see Butterflies in Stirlingshire

1. Wester Moss and Polmaise Bing, Fallin

(NS837913). OS Landranger 57, 58, Explorer 366

A sparsely vegetated coal bing with scrub that attracts Common Blue and Six-spot Burnet moths. Numbers of butterflies can vary depending on the Birdsfoot-trefoil population which can get almost eaten out of existence. The adjacent Wester Moss Bog is a good site to see Large Heath but care needs to be taken as all bog sites are potentially dangerous due to the hidden water filled ditches in the peat.

Target Species: Large Heath and Common Blue.

Parking: Park by the Colliery memorial at NS 840914.

Polmaise Bing, Fallin

Large Heath

Flanders Moss

2. Flanders Moss NNR

(NS636972). OS Landranger 57 Explorer 365

National Nature Reserve and Scottish Wildlife Trust Reserve, on the boundary between vice counties 86 and 87.

Access is currently restricted to open days, and permission from SWT or SNH due to reasons of safety. An access route is at present under consideration to allow public access (more information from Scottish Natural Heritage).

Target Species: Large Heath and Green Hairstreak

Stirlingshire

Mugdock Country Park – a variety of habitats are present including heathland

Green Hairstreak on Blaeberry

3. Mugdock Country Park

(NS5577). OS Landranger 64, Explorer 348

Woodland, grassland and heath

Target Species: Small Pearl-bordered Fritillary, Purple Hairstreak and Common Blue. Green Hairstreak at Drumclog Muir (NS550759).

Other Species: Green-veined White, Orange-tip, Common Blue, Small Copper, Small Tortoiseshell, Ringlet, Meadow Brown and Small Heath.

Parking: Large Car Park, visitor centre and toilets at NS546779. Also the Kyber Car Park (NS542774). Access is via the A81 and is well signposted from the junction south of Loch Ardinning at NS566771.

4. Loch Ardinning

(NS564779). OS Landranger 64, Explorer 348

Scottish Wildlife Trust Reserve. Open water, woodland, heath and marsh.

Target species: Green Hairstreak and Small Pearl-bordered Fritillary.

Other Species: Green-veined White, Orange-tip, Common Blue and Red-necked Footman Moth.

Parking: Park at the lay-by located off the A81 near Strathblane and Milngavie at NS564778.

5. Palacerigg Country Park, Cumbernauld

(NS786733). OS Landranger 64, Explorer 349

Woodland and meadows

Target Species: Small Pearl-bordered Fritillary and Green Hairstreak.

Other species: Large White, Small White, Green-veined White, Orange-tip, Small Copper, Common Blue, Small Tortoiseshell, Peacock, Dark Green Fritillary, Meadow Brown, Ringlet and Small Heath.

Parking: Large car park with visitor centre and toilets.

6. Burnside Wood, Kippen

(NS6594). OS Landranger 57, Explorer 348

Part of a local walk and nature trail. Cross the Common and football field to reach the wood. Kippen overlooks the Forth Valley and beautiful scenery.

Target Species: Orange-tip and Ringlet.

Other species: Green-veined White, Small Tortoiseshell, Peacock, Red Admiral, Painted Lady, Meadow Brown, Ringlet.

Parking: Park in Kippen.

7. Cashel

(NS4094). OS Landranger 56, Explorer 347/364

Woodland Walk with fine views of Loch Lomond.

Target Species: Scotch Argus, Green Hairstreak and Small Pearl-bordered Fritillary.

Other species: Large White, Small White, Green-veined White, Orange-tip, Small Copper, Common Blue, Red Admiral, Painted Lady, Small Tortoiseshell, Peacock, Dark Green Fritillary, Meadow Brown, Ringlet and Small Heath.

Parking: North of Balmaha, park at NS400941.

A male Purple Hairstreak. A strong population of the Purple Hairstreak is located on the eastern side of Loch Lomond

8. Sallochy

(NS387951). OS Landranger 56, Explorer 364

Oak woodland located beside Loch Lomond and on the route of the West Highland Way.

Target Species: Purple Hairstreak.

Parking: Park at Forestry Commission Car Park NS380958 then walk to oaks at NS387951.

Butterfly Conservation Scotland has produced a very useful leaflet, *Butterflies of Lomond and Rural Stirling – an identification guide*, which illustrates all the butterflies found in Stirlingshire and some of the better butterfly sites.

Stirlingshire

Argyll and the Isles
(Vice Counties 98, 100, 101, 102 and 103)

ARGYLL and the Isles make up an area of Scotland that has a stunningly beautiful landscape and a wide diversity of habitats. These range from an extensive dune and machair system on the islands, at sea level, to some of the finest arctic-alpine environments in Britain on the inland mountains. There are also important areas of raised bog, valley mire, herb-rich flushed meadows and native deciduous woodland. The Clyde Isles and Arran add further interest. The long coastline of Argyll comprises raised beaches and coastal cliff, and screes which often create sun-traps and support a wide variety of nectaring flowers and larval food plants.

The coastline of Mull alone is over 300 miles long. Wherever there are south facing crumbling slopes between basalt cliffs there are rich assemblages of herb-rich grasslands providing warm suntraps and ideal nectaring and breeding grounds for a wide range of butterflies such as Common Blue and Grayling, and attractive day flying moths, such as the Burnet Moths.

The island of Lismore consists of limestone, and although the soil is in short supply its name 'the big garden' is well deserved for there is an abundance of wild flowers. Similar limestone outcrops occur throughout Appin. The Marsh Fritillary and Orange-tip are present in moist meadows between the limestone outcrops.

Between Loch Etive in the north and Ardfern, in mid Argyll, rolling volcanic andesite hills extend eastwards until they meet up with the unfertile granite mass of Cruachan and the rich arctic-alpine communities on the schists of Beinn Laoigh (Ben Lui), home to the Mountain Ringlet. The make-up of the ground results in favourable microclimates and enriched soil conditions which support some of the richest insect life in Scotland. The heathland and moorland support Large Heath butterflies and the herb-rich flushed meadows are important for Green-veined White, Orange-tip and Small Pearl-bordered Fritillary as well as the grassland species, Meadow Brown, Small Heath and Scotch Argus.

The extensive Oak woodlands which together with the coastal Hazel woods and substantial Birch woods, Alder swamp and Sallow carr, provide niches for some of the rarest British butterflies. These include the Chequered Skipper, Marsh Fritillary and Pearl-bordered Fritillary, which all favour sheltered sunny glades and south facing bays at the edges of woods. Although a species exclusive to Oak, the Purple Hairstreak is by no means ubiquitous in Argyll's extensive Oak forests. It seems to prefer trees with substantial crowns in sunny but sheltered situations.

Atlantic Hazel woods, examples of which can be found on Lismore, Kerrera, Seil and Mull, as well as coastal localities on the mainland, are unique examples of what must be one of the oldest woodland formations in Britain. They are largely unaltered since the first Hazel nuts were washed ashore and took root above the high tide mark soon after the ice of the last great glaciation disappeared 10,000 years ago. Where these woods appear on a south-facing aspect such as at Ballachuan Scottish Wildlife Trust

Mountain Ringlet, a butterfly of the mountains, such as Beinn Laoigh (Ben Lui)

Reserve, south of Oban, they provide ideal conditions for butterflies such as the Speckled Wood, while alternating wet and dry meadows between the Hazel patches support strong populations of Common Blue, Small Heath, Meadow Brown, Scotch Argus, Grayling, Dark Green Fritillary, Small Pearl-bordered Fritillary and Marsh Fritillary.

Argyll still supports more native deciduous woodland than any other region in Scotland, despite the widespread commercial coniferisation which has taken place over the past fifty years. Blanket planting with conifers has resulted in the loss and fragment-ation of many butterfly populations with Pearl-bordered Fritillary and Marsh Fritillary being among the worst affected. However as these forests reach harvesting age there is an unprecedented opportunity for their restructuring to provide ideal butterfly habitat, with a network of clearings linked by wide corridors along forest roads, rides and wayleaves. An optimum of 25-30m width is required to avoid excess shading as the trees grow. Such gaps are also essential along water courses, in areas bordering broadleaved woodland and on the southern edge of woodland. Chequered Skipper, Pearl-bordered Fritillary, Small Pearl-bordered Fritillary and Marsh Fritillary particularly benefit from such measures.

A recent addition to Argyll is the Orange-tip which first appeared at Corran Ferry in the mid 1980s. By 1990 it had moved south to colonise Glasdrum NNR, Barcaldine and Benderloch peninsular and is now widespread in coastal districts. Argyll was the northern limit of the Peacock but it has increased its numbers and extended its range since 2000 and is now found even further north. Migrants periodically reaching Argyll include Clouded Yellow, Red Admiral and Painted Lady.

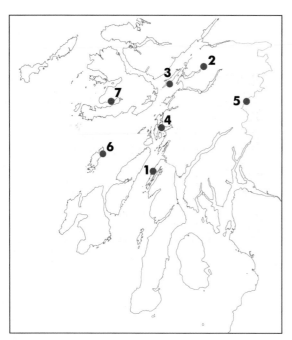

Location of butterfly sites in Argyll

1. Taynish National Nature Reserve

2. Glasdrum National Nature Reserve

3. Lismore Island

4. Ballachuan Hazel Woods, Scottish Wildlife Trust Reserve

5. Beinn Laoigh (Ben Lui)

6. Coille Mor, Colonsay

7. South Ardmeanach coast, Uamh nam Muc (NM4827) to The Wilderness (NM4029), Isle of Mull

Speckled Wood *oblita* subspecies
(Faery Isles, Knapdale, NR7789)

Argyll and the Isles butterfly sites

1. Taynish National Nature Reserve
(NR7385). OS Landranger 55, Explorer 358

Taynish is one of the finest woodland National Nature Reserves in Scotland, supporting the largest area of Oak woodland surviving in the extensively coniferised Knapdale region in mid Argyll. Valley mires also support rich and diverse communities of invertebrates and flora including reed beds, Sharp-flowered Rush meadow, grassland, marshes, peatland and fen running along the central valley. Bar Mor is a rocky ridge of Dalradian schist above the wind sloped Oak woods.

Target Species: Marsh Fritillary, Green Hairstreak, Speckled Wood and Large Heath.

Other Species: Green-veined White, Common Blue, Small Copper, Small Tortoiseshell, Peacock, Red Admiral, Scotch Argus, Grayling, Meadow Brown, Small Heath.

Parking: Car park south of lochan at (NR737852). A picnic area is also present.

Taynish National Nature Reserve

2. Glasdrum National Nature Reserve
(NN0045). OS Landranger 49/50, Explorer 384/376

Glasdrum NNR consists of a south-easterly facing hanging wood on the steep slopes of Glen Creran. The lower slopes consist mainly of Ash and Alder woodland with lime rich soils supporting a rich ground flora. Higher up the hill, on acidic soils, Oak is dominant with a Blaeberry ground cover. Open glades support herb-rich flushed communities, Sharp-flowered Rush meadows and Purple Moor-grass tussocks. On the upper edge of the tree line the Oak gives way to Birch.

Target Species: Chequered Skipper, Pearl-bordered Fritillary, Small Pearl-bordered Fritillary, Green Hairstreak and Mountain Ringlet (on upper slopes above the tree line).

Other Species: Green-veined White, Orange-tip, Small Copper, Dark Green Fritillary, Peacock, Painted Lady, Speckled Wood, Scotch Argus, Meadow Brown, Ringlet and Small Heath.

Parking: Two miles east of the Creagan Bridge and the A828 is a car park and picnic site at NM997452.

Glasdrum National Nature Reserve. Butterfly Conservation field trip, May 2005, looking for Chequered Skipper

3. Lismore Island

(NM 8239). OS Landranger 49, Explorer 376

Lismore consists of limestone and although the soil is thin, there is an abundance of wild flowers such as Common Rock-rose. In contrast there is also some acid heath habitat over the limestone. Marsh Fritillary can be found in almost any suntrap marshy location across the Island. One of the best colonies is along the track to Port Ramsay in the north.

Target Species: Marsh Fritillary

Other Species: Green-veined White, Small Copper, Common Blue, Peacock and Small Heath. Grayling used to be abundant here but they seem to have suffered a recent decline.

Access: There is a car ferry from Oban to Achnacroish (NM8540) and a small passenger ferry runs from Port Appin to The Point in the north of the island (NM8946).

4. Ballachuan Hazel Woods, Scottish Wildlife Trust Reserve

(NM7614). OS Landranger 55, Explorer 359

This is a very fine example of Atlantic Hazel wood and one of the most ancient woodland types in Britain.

Target Species: Marsh Fritillary

Other Species: Green-veined White, Common Blue, Small Pearl-bordered Fritillary, Speckled Wood, Small Heath and Meadow Brown.

Parking/access: Access from Cuan where the ferry crosses to Luing.

5. Beinn Laoigh (Ben Lui)

(NN2626). OS Landranger 50, Explorer 377

Ben Laoigh rises to 1130m and has rich assemblages of arctic-alpine vegetation on crags of Moine schist. Mountain Ringlet has been recorded from the slopes to the west and south-west of the main peak.

Target Species: Mountain Ringlet

Parking/access: Car park at NN238278 by the A85 in Glen Lochy. A track runs from here through Sitka Spruce plantation to Fionn Choirer.

6. Coille Mor, Colonsay

(NR4196). OS Landranger 61, Explorer 354

This site has wind-shaped ancient Oak woodland on Torridonian sandstone on the south-eastern side of Beinn nam Fitheach. It is a site that is known to have a rich butterfly fauna but was under recorded due to remoteness. For example, Purple Hairstreak was not recorded from Colonsay during the survey period because the site was not visited during the appropriate time of year. Few of the Oaks are more than 5m high allowing good views of the usually elusive Purple Hairstreak in the Oak canopy. Small rills flow down seepage hollows formed by the bedrock supporting interesting botanical communities. Ringlet is near its north western limit. Fritillaries are found in the little valley on the south side of the wood.

Target Species: Purple Hairstreak, Ringlet.

Other Species: Green-veined White, Common Blue, Marsh Fritillary, Small Pearl-bordered Fritillary, Dark Green Fritillary, Grayling and Meadow Brown.

Access: Cross country east from Kiloran or north along the coast from Scalasaig.

7. South Ardmeanach coast, Uamh nam Muc (NM4827) to The Wilderness (NM4029), Isle of Mull

OS Landranger 48, Explorer 373/375

This stretch of south-facing coastline provides extensive herb-rich suntrap conditions. Thyme heath and grassland combine with Bracken on the deeper soils around the Burg and to the east. To the west, steep unstable coastal screes between basalt crags and the shore support rich maritime vegetation with an abundance of Thyme and Birds-foot Trefoil. In addition to their importance for butterflies these slopes also support important moth populations.

Target Species: Dark Green Fritillary, Common Blue and Small Heath.

Other species: Red Admiral, Small Tortoiseshell, Peacock, Speckled Wood, Scotch Argus, Grayling and Meadow Brown.

Access: National Trust for Scotland car park at NM477275. A rough road runs to the Burg.

Ardmeanach coast, Isle of Mull

Marsh Fritillary mating pair, the female is on the left. The Marsh Fritillary
is a highlight of the Lepidoptera fauna in Argyll

Table 4 Scientific names of Plants mentioned in the text

Alder	*Alnus glutinosa*	Holly	*Ilex aquifolium*
Alder Buckthorn	*Frangula alnus*	Honesty	*Lunaria annua*
Aubrietia	*Aubrietia deltoides*	Hybrid Butterfly Bush	*Buddleia x weyeriana*
Bell Heather	*Erica cinerea*	Ice Plant 'Autumn Joy'	*Sedum spectabile*
Birch	*Betula spp.*	Incense Bush	*Eupatorium ligustrinum*
Birdsfoot-trefoil	*Lotus corniculatus*	Hop	*Humulus lupulus*
Blackthorn	*Prunus spinosa*	Ivy	*Hedera helix*
Blaeberry	*Vaccinium myrtillus*	Kidney Vetch	*Anthyllis vulneraria*
Bloody Cranesbill	*Geranium sanguineum*	Lesser Knapweed	*Centaurea nigra*
Bluebell	*Endymion non-scriptus*	Marjoram	*Origanum vulgare*
Bog Myrtle	*Myrica gale*	Marsh Cudweed	*Gnaphalium uliginosum*
Bracken	*Pteridium aquilinum*	Marsh Thistle	*Cirsium palustre*
Bramble	*Rubus fruticosus agg.*	Marsh Violet	*Viola palustris*
Buckthorn	*Rhamnus cartharticus*	Mat-grass	*Nardus stricta*
Buddleia	*Buddleia davidii*	Michaelmas Daisy	*Aster novi-belgii*
Bugle	*Ajuga reptans*	Mint	*Mentha spp.*
Cabbage	*Brassica oleracea*	Narrow Buckler Fern	*Dryopteris cathusiana*
Catsear	*Hypochaeris radicata*	Orange Ball Butterfly Bush	*Buddleia globosa*
Cock's-foot	*Dactylis glomerata*	Pedunculate Oak	*Quercus robur*
Common Bent	*Agrostis capillaris*	Purpletop Verbena	*Verbena bonariensis*
Common Dog Violet	*Viola riviniana*	Pussy Willow	*Salix spp.*
Common Rock-rose	*Helianthemum nummularium*	Ragwort	*Senecio jacobaea*
Common Sorrel	*Rumex acetosa*	Red Clover	*Trifolium pratense*
Couch	*Elymus repens*	Red Fescue	*Festuca rubra*
Cowberry	*Vaccinium vitis-idaea*	Royal Fern	*Osmunda regalis*
Cranberry	*Vaccinium oxycoccos*	Rosebay Willowherb	*Epilobium angustifolium*
Creeping Buttercup	*Ranunculus repens*	Sea Radish	*Raphanus raphanistrum maritimus*
Creeping Thistle	*Cirsium arvense*	Sessile Oak	*Quercus petraea*
Cross-leaved Heath	*Erica tetralix*	Sheep's Fescue	*Festuca ovina agg.*
Crowberry	*Empetrum nigrum agg.*	Sheep's Sorrel	*Rumex acetosella*
Cuckoo Flower	*Cardamine pratensis*	Sitka Spruce	*Picea sitchensis*
Daisy	*Bellis perennis*	Smooth Meadow-grass	*Poa pratensis*
Dame's Violet	*Hesperis matronalis*	Soft Rush	*Juncus effusus*
Dandelion	*Taraxacum spp.*	Spear Thistle	*Cirsium vulgare*
Devil's-bit Scabious	*Succisa pratensis*	Stinging Nettle	*Urtica dioica*
Dove's-foot Cranesbill	*Geranium molle*	Sycamore	*Acer pseudoplatanus*
Forget-me-not	*Myosotis spp.*	Thrift	*Armeria maritima*
Garden Nasturtium	*Tropaeolum majus*	Thyme	*Thymus serpyllum agg*
Garlic Mustard	*Alliaria petiolata*	Tormentil	*Potentilla erecta*
Greater Birdsfoot-trefoil	*Lotus uliginosus*	Tufted Hair-grass	*Deschampsia cespitosa*
Greater Butterfly Orchid	*Platanthera chlorantha*	Tufted Vetch	*Vicia cracca*
Gorse	*Ulex europaeus*	Valerian	*Valeriana officinalis*
Harebell	*Campanula rotundifolia*	Wavy Hair-grass	*Deschampsia flexuosa*
Hare's-tail Cotton-grass	*Eriophorum vaginatum*	White Clover	*Trifolium repens*
Hazel	*Corylus avellana*	Whored Caraway	*Carum verticillatum*
Heath Bedstraw	*Galium saxatile*	Wild Angelica	*Angelica sylvestris*
Heath Dog Violet	*Viola canina*	Wild Pansy	*Viola tricolor*
Heath Spotted Orchid	*Dactylorhiza maculata*	Wych Elm	*Ulmus glabra*
Heather	*Calluna vulgaris*		

Further Reading

Historical Records

Thomson, G. (1980) *The Butterflies of Scotland – a natural history* Croom Helm. London.
George Thomson's classic work provides a detailed historical account of the butterflies of Scotland up to the late 1970s.

Field Guide

Lewington, R. (2003) *Pocket Guide to the Butterflies of Great Britain and Ireland*. British Wildlife Publishing.
The best field guide available which neatly fits the pocket.

Photographic Guide

Tomlinson, D. and Still, R. (2002). Britain's Butterflies. Wild Guides Ltd.
Photographic summary of all the butterflies found in Britain including pictures of the egg, caterpillar and chrysalis.

Porter, J. (1997). The Colour Identification Guide to Caterpillars of the British Isles. Viking.

General Reading

Asher, J., Warren, M., Fox, R., Harding, P., Jeffcoate, G. and Jeffcoate, S. (2001). *The Millennium Atlas of Butterflies in Britain and Ireland*. Oxford University Press.
Summary of butterfly distributions from the five year national survey (1995-1999).

Thomas, J. and Lewington, R. (1991). *The Butterflies of Britain & Ireland*. Dorling Kindersley in assoc. with the National Trust.
Superb commentary and beautiful illustrations.

Emmet, A.M. and Heath, J. (ed) (1990). *The moths and butterflies of Great Britain and Ireland, 7 part 1*, Hesperiidae-Nymphalidae, the butterflies. Harley Books, Colchester. (Pbk edition revised with minor corrections).
Part of an encyclopaedic reference of the British Lepidoptera, recommended.

Emmet, A.M. (1991) *The Scientific Names of the British Lepidoptera their history and meaning* Harley Books.

Harmer, A.S. (2000) *Variation in British Butterflies* Paphia Publishing Ltd.

Mitchell, J. (2001). *Loch Lomondside* The New Naturalist. Harper Collins.

Butterfly Conservation booklets

Ravenscroft, N. (1996) *The Chequered Skipper*.
Tucker, M. (1997) *The Red Admiral Butterfly*.
Willmott, K. (1999). *The Holly Blue Butterfly*.

References

Barnett, L.K. & Warren, M.S. (1995) *Marsh Fritillary Species Action Plan* Butterfly Conservation unpublished report.

Brereton, T. , Roy, D. & Greatorix-Davies, N. (2006) 'Thirty years and counting. The contribution to conservation and ecology of butterfly-monitoring in the UK.' *British Wildlife* 17, 162-170.

Cunningham, D. (1950). '*Celastrina argiolus* in Scotland (Dumfriesshire)' *Entomologist* 83, 235.

Futter, K. (1993) 'Ringlets in the Clyde Valley', *On the Spot* newsletter of Glasgow and South West Scotland Branch of Butterfly Conservation. **12** 1993, 5-6.

Futter, S. and Futter, K. (1998) 'The successful colonisation of the Brucehill Cliff Local Nature Reserve, Dumbarton, by Orange Tip butterflies *Anthocharis cardamines*'. *The Glasgow Naturalist* 23, 63-64.

Gaston, K.J., Smith, R.M., Thompson, K. & Warren, P. (2004) 'Gardens and Wildlife – the BUGS project'. *British Wildlife* 16, 1-9.

Heath, J., Pollard, E. & Thomas, J.A. (1984) *Atlas of Butterflies in Britain and Ireland* Viking.

Holland, J. (2000) 'Mountain Ringlet Species Action Plan'. Scottish Agricultural College and Upland Working Group.

Kinnear, P. & Kirkland, P. (2000) 'Regional Action Plan for the Butterflies and Moths of South West Scotland'. Butterfly Conservation, Stirling.

Kirkland, P. (2005) 'The Scotch Argus'. *Butterfly*, the magazine of Butterfly Conservation. **89**, 23-25.

Marren, P. (2004) 'The English names of butterflies'. *British Wildlife* 15, 401-408.

Mitchell, J. (2003) 'Loch Lomond and the Trossachs National Park'. *British Wildlife* 14, 340-348.

Perring, F.H. & Walters, S.M. (Eds.). (1990) *Atlas of the British Flora*. Botanical Society of the British Isles.

Preston, C.D., Pearman, D.A. & Dines, T.D. (Eds.). (2002) *The New Atlas of the British and Irish Flora* Oxford University Press.

Sutcliffe, R. (1991) 'Scottish Butterfly Report 1988-1990'. Unpublished report by the Glasgow & South-West Scotland Branch of Butterfly Conservation.

Sutcliffe, R. (1994). 'The Clouded Yellow Invasion of Scotland, 1992'. *The Glasgow Naturalist* 22, 389-396.

Sutcliffe, R. and Kirkland, P. (1998). 'The Spread of the Orange Tip in Scotland (1998)'. *The Glasgow Naturalist* 23, 64-65.

Zonfrillo, B & Hancock, E.G. (2004) 'Abundance and patterns of occurrence in butterflies from Ailsa Craig, Ayrshire'. *The Glasgow Naturalist* 23, 137-140.

Useful Contacts and Societies

Butterfly Conservation – Glasgow & South West Scotland Branch
Chairman: David Welham Web site : www.southwestscotland-butterflies.org.uk
Butterfly Conservation, Scotland
Contact: Balallan House, Allan Park, Stirling FK8 2QG
Tel: 0870 7706151 Web site: www.butterfly-conservation.org/bcuk/scotland
Butterfly Conservation Headquarters
Manor Yard, East Lulworth, Wareham, Dorset BH20 5QP
Tel: 0870 774 4309 Web site: www.butterfly-conservation.org

Scottish Wildlife Trust Headquarters
Cramond House, Kirk Cramond,
Cramond Glebe Road, Edinburgh EH4 6NS
Tel: 0131 312 7765 Web site: www.swt.org.uk

Scottish Natural Heritage Headquarters
12 Hope Terrace, Edinburgh EH9 2AS
Tel: 0131 447 4784 Web site: www.snh.org.uk

Loch Lomond & The Trossachs National Park Headquarters
The Old Station, Balloch Road, Balloch G83 8BF
Tel: 01389 722 600 Web site: www.lochlomond.trossachs.org

National Trust for Scotland Headquarters
Wemyss House, 28 Charlotte Square, Edinburgh EH2 4ET
Tel: 0131 243 9300 Web site: www.nts.org.uk

Photographic Acknowledgements

T. Norman Tait: Front cover, 4, 6, 26, 27, 30, 37, 40, 44, 48, 50, 58, 60, 61, 64, 66, 68, 72, 76, 80, 83, 88, 91, 95 bottom left, 101 top left, 108, 115, 119 right bottom, 128, 129, 131, 132, 138 top, 145, 149 bottom, Back cover top.
Jim Black: 21, 25, 34, 38, 42 left, 46, 57, 69, 73, 84, 86, 94 bottom, 96, 98, 102 top right, 103 top left, 114 bottom, 117, 121, 122, 123, 125, 126, 136, 143, 146, 147 top.
Richard Sutcliffe: 7, 11, 13, 15, 16, 18, 28, 32, 36 left, 39, 54, 56, 90 left, 94 top, 100, 103 bottom, 107 right, 116, 127, 130 top, 130 bottom left, 133, 141 middle, 142, 160, Back cover bottom.
Keith Futter: 9, 12, 35, 36 right, 42 right, 47, 55, 62 left, 70, 78, 82, 85, 93, 95 top left, 95 bottom right, 97 bottom, 101 bottom, 102 top left, bottom, 105, 106 left, 107 left, 109, 110, 112, 134, 135, 137, 138 middle, bottom, 139, 144.
Jim McCleary: 95 top right, 97 top, 99, 103 top right, 106 right, 118 bottom, 119 top, 119 left bottom, 120 top, 124, 130 bottom right, 141 bottom, 149 top.
Gerry Rodway: 17, 19, 29, 52, 62 right, 74, 92,101 top right.
Jessie McKay: 23, 118 top. **Neil Gregory**: 114 top, back cover flap bottom.
David Welham: 141 top, 147 bottom. **Gordon Riddle**: 90 right. **R.G. Stevens**: 63, 102.
Susan Futter: 113. **Graham Smith**: 120 bottom. **John Mitchell**: 140.

Acknowledgements

THE AUTHORS would like to especially thank Jim Asher and Richard Fox for all their help at a national level, and Chris Stamp, Jeff Waddell and David Barbour (recorders for East Scotland and Highland branches). We would also like to thank the staff of Butterfly Conservation at the head office at Wareham Dorset, in particular Georgie Laing, Lester Cowling and Sandra Muldoon for assistance with queries.

Many people have provided their expert knowledge and general assistance and we particularly thank John Halliday, Nick Holding, Morag Mackinnon, Richard and Barbara Mearns, David Robertson, Geoff Shaw, Graham Smith, Sheilagh Stewart and Peter Wormwell.

We thank Dr Mark Shaw and Dr Keith Porter for providing information on caterpillar parasites.

We reserve special thanks to Derek Rodger of Argyll Publishing for his enthusiasm and support for this book project.

We gratefully acknowledge the financial support in producing this book provided by the Lottery Awards for All, Scottish Natural Heritage, Blodwen Lloyd Binns Bequest Fund (administered by the Glasgow Natural History Society), Royal Bank of Scotland Community Cashback Scheme and funding from the Glasgow & South West Scotland branch of Butterfly Conservation.

The photographic images used in this book were provided by T. Norman Tait, Jim Black, Richard Sutcliffe, Keith Futter, Jim McCleary, Jessie MacKay, David Welham, Neil Gregory, Susan Futter, John Michell, Graham Smith, Gordon Riddle and R.G. Stevens.

The phenograms were produced from *Levana* and the maps were produced by *MapMate* using Digital Map Data © Bartholomew 2002.

Most importantly, this book would not have been possible without the support of all the organisations and individual recorders who have contributed anything from single records to as many as 9874 records over the ten year period. The terrain of South West Scotland can be difficult to access in the remote and upland areas but through dedication and commitment nearly every 5km square was covered, although butterflies may not have been seen in every 5km square. The names of the recorders are listed below. We apologise if we have missed anyone and for errors.

Arran Ranger Service, Ayrshire Bird Report, Butterfly Monitoring Scheme, Biological Recording in Scotland, Brodick Country Park Ranger Service, British Trust for Ornithology, Clyde Muirshiel Regional Park Ranger Service, CARSE, Drumpellier Country Park Rangers, East Ayrshire Countryside Ranger Service, Highland Biological Recording Group, North Lanarkshire Conservation & Greening, Conservation Section, Glasgow City Council Ranger Service, Glasgow Museums Biological Records Centre, Gleniffer Braes Ranger Service, National Trust for Scotland, Inverness Museum

Records Centre, Paisley Museum Natural History Society, Palacerigg Country Park, Royal Society for the Protection of Birds, Scottish Environmental Protection Agency, Scottish Natural Heritage, South Lanarkshire Ranger Service, Stirling Ranger Service, Scottish Wildlife Trust, Tullie House Records, and pupils of Mosshead, Bearsden and Dalry Primary Schools

Barry Ackers, Aileen Adam, Andrew Adam, Ian Adams, Prof Roger Adams, S. Adams, Craig Addies, W. Addies, Hugh Addlesee, John Aiken, Mrs M. Airley, C.I. Aitchison, Margaret Aitchison, Carol Aitken, Frank Albert, Liz Albert, S.T.E. Aldhouse, Keith Alexander, Debbie Allan, Elspeth Allan, Morag Allan, Shona Allan, Caroline Allen, Miss Jane Allen, L. Allen, Mrs Allen, Ian Amatt, Mr Amos, Mr Anderson, Mrs Anderson, Dr Angus Anderson, Mrs Maureen Anderson, W.W. Anderson, I. Andrew, Peter Andrews, Tristan Ap Rheinallt, Mr E. Archer, Douglas Armour, Jean Armstrong, Brian Arneill, Jim Asher, Jenn & Ian Atkin, Catherine Atkins, Mrs R.J. Austin, Maurice Avent, A.B.G. & A.M. Averis, Jonathan Ayres,
N. Bacciu, John S. Bailey, Patrick Bailley, Ann Baird, Sheila Baird, Margaret F. Baister, Dan Baker, Paul Baker, N. Balchock, Janice Bald, N. Baldock, Chris Balling, Dr D. A. Barbour, T. Barbour, J. Barclay, A.J.&l.J. Barker, Mike Barnham, David Barr, Ms F.A. Barratt, Mrs V. Barrie, John Bartle,
Mrs J.E. Bartlett, Elizabeth Bastow, Mary Bates, Pat Batty, Judy Baxter, Mrs T. Beal, R.A. Beatty, S. Beck, Roy Bedford, Anna Bell, Dr D. Bell, Mike Bell, A. Bennie, John Bennie, Nancy Bent, Mr F.R. Bentley, Sheila Bett, C. Bettison, Helen Bibby, Jonathan Bills, Margaret Binks, Mr Birrell, David Black, Dr James P Black, Laura Black, D. Black, F. Black, Mrs Black, Judith Blackwell, Angus Blair, Andrew Blake, Dr Keith Bland, John Blane, Paul Blount, Adam G Boggon, Ian Boler, Ken Bond, William Bonner, D. Booth, L. Borradaile, Carole Bottomley, Mrs Elizabeth Bowen, Mrs Frances L. Bowie, David Bowker, Peter Bowle, Colin Bowler,

John Bowler, Christopher E. Bowly, Charles Boyle, Helen Boyle, John Boyle, Mrs Marjory Boyle, Jean A. Boynton, W.R. Brackenridge, Steve Bradley, Michael J Bradley, Alan Bradshaw, Mike Braid, E.H. Braid, Mark Brand, Simon Breasley, Tom Brereton, Mrs E.S. Briggs, Roger Bristow, Roger Broad, Ailsa Brockie, J Bromley, Calum Brookes, Tony Brotherton, Alan Brown, Lesley Brown, Doug A. Brown, Mrs Helen Brown, Isabel Brown, Mr Rory Brown, R.M. Brown, Tom Brown, W.R.M. Brown, Mrs Brownlee, Chloe Bruce, Jennifer Bruce,
Mr Bruges, Mrs E. Bruin, Mrs M. Brunt, Mr Bryson, Alex Buchanan, Richard Buckland, Mr B. Bullen, Anne Burgess, Mrs E. Burnett, T. Burniston, Mrs Betty Burns, Ian Burrus, C. Bush, K. Butterworth, A.R. Buttery,
Miss P.A. Caldwell, Stephen Callaghan, C.M. Cameron, E. D Cameron, Euan Cameron, Mr Cameron, Mrs Anne Campbell, Mrs Audrey Campbell, Glen Campbell, Graeme Campbell, Jonathan Campbell, Laura Campbell, Oscar Campbell, R. Campbell, Robert J. Campbell, Mrs Sandra Campbell, John Candlish, C.P. Canfield, J. Cann, Wm. H. Cant, Ian Carballo, Stuart Carle, Bryony Carnie, Lena Carroll, Mrs Sheila Carson, Anne Carstairs, Paul G. Carter, Hebe L. Carus, Andrew Cassels, Graeme Cathcart, Peter Cawley,
E. Chadfield, Mr Chalmers, P. Chennery, Mrs Yvonne Chester, Claire Chisem, H Chisholm, G. Christie, Ian Christie, Janet Christie, Mrs Jane Christie, Mrs Sena Christie, Mr Churches, Mrs M. Cinderey, Joanna Cindiskis, Gail Cisman, Dr Clapham, Hugh Clark, Ian Clark, M. Clark, Miss M.R. Clark, Mrs Clark, Mrs P.M. Clark, Toni Clark, Dr J.H. Clarke, Thomas Clarkson, Jean Clayworth, L. Clehane, S. Cleland, David L. Clugston, Mrs Margaret Clyde, Ellen Clydesdale, S Cobb, A. & I. Cochrane, Bob Cole, F Cole, Barry & Jennifer Collett, David Collie, M.J.G. Collie, Paul N. Collin, Martin Collinson, Mr K.D. Connock, A.M. Cook, Lyndsay Cook, Tim D. Cook, N.H. Cooke, P. Cool, David Cooling, David Cooper, Karen Corley, Charles Corser, Iris Cotgrove, Lorna

Cottingham, Mr R. Cottis, James Cowan, Ana Cox, Julian Cox, Jim Coyle, Nancy Craib, A. Craig, Jean Craig, Peter Cramb, George Crawshaw, John Cree, Mrs S.E. Cressey, Jim Cropper, Betty Crowson, Mr Cumberford, Alan Cumming, Mrs E. Cumming, Richard Cumming, Ian R. Cunningham, T.P. Cunningham,

Nick Dadds, Andrew Dalgleish, Georgina Dalton, R.H. Daly, H. Dalzell, Mary Dalzell, Ronald Dalziel, Joe Damiel, Tom Daniels, Anthony Darby, J. Darby, W. Darby, Anne Davidson, Bill Davidson, Iain Davidson, M.S. Davidson, Mrs Caryl A. Davidson, Stuart Davidson, W. Davidson, Wilma Davidson, Mark Davies, Sally Davies, E.C. & J.M. Davies, A. Davis, J.A. Davis, Andrew Daw, Paul Daw, J. Dawson, Mr M.W. Dawson, Mrs J. Dawson, Miss Marika De Pettes, Janet Dearie, M.B. Dempster, Matthew Denes, David Dennis, Mr D. Dennis, A.R. Devlin, Mrs E.P. Dewar, G. Diack, Ian Diack, Emilio Dicerbo, Eric Dickie, Mr A. Dickson, Camilla Dickson, John Dickson, Austin Dobbs, Ruth Dobson, Mr Dogood, Mrs Donaldson, Lindsay Door, Miss C. Dougal, Pat Doughty, Ewan Douglas, Mrs Lesley Douglas, Mr A Dowell, A.J. Downie, Lesley Dron, Mary Jane Leighton Dryburgh, Jeanette Drysdale, Dr I. Duncan, James Duncan, Miss Patti Duncan, Mrs E. Duncan, A. Duncombe, A.L.M. Dunn, G.M. Dunn, Mrs E.T. Dunn, Jeff Dunn, L.F. Dunse, Mrs Sheena Dunsmore, Mr B. Dyson,

Muriel Eadie, Simon R. Eccles, Mr Eckersall, A. Edgar, Mrs J. Edwards, K. Egerton, Helge Engelking, Sarah Eno, Ian Evans, Mrs L.J.K. Evans, V.M. Ewens, D. Eyre,

G. Fairbairn, Joanne Falconer, Mrs Farr, Colin Farrell, Lynne Farrell, David Farrow, Alex Faulds, M. Featherstone, Helen Fenby, Anne Fergus, Ian D. Ferguson, Maggie Ferguson, Mrs Ferguson, Mrs Janet Fiander, Allan Finlayson, Rev Duncan Finlayson, Anne Fisher, Stan Fisher, S. Fisk , Fiona Fleming, Mr Fleming, Frank Fleming, Ian Fleming, John Fleming, Mrs Mary Forbes, Mrs M.M. Ford, Marjory Foreman, Gavin Forest, E.

Forrest, Simon Forrest, Kate Foster, Neil Foster, D.M. Fowler, D. Fowler, Richard Fox, Aldina Franco, E. Fraser, F.C. Fraser, Margaret Fraser, Jim Frew, J. & K. Fulford, Mike Fuller, Roy Fussell, Dr Keith Futter, Susan Futter, Dr G.J. Fyfe, Gillian Fyfe,

David Galbraith, Mrs Elizabeth Gamble, Doreen Gardner, Miss L.S. Garrad, Dennis Garratt, Mrs R. Garrod, K. Gartside, Yvonne Gauld, M. Gaywood, Barbara Geller, Eileen M. Gemmill, A. Gibson, Iain P. Gibson, Mr J.A. Gibson, Dr J.A. Gibson , James Gibson, Jennie Campbell Gibson, Maisie Gibson, Mariona Gibson, Mrs Gibson, Stuart Gibson, J. Gilbert, Tony Gilbert, L. Gill, Francis Gillan, Jackie Gillespie, Mr Ed Gillett, M. Gillett, James M. Girvin, Adam Giselah, David Given, Stuart Glen, Andy Godfrey, Alison S. Goldie, Adrian Goodhand, Mrs G. Gordon, Ken Gouge, Mrs Carol Govan, Valerie S. Govan, Dr Stuart Graham, B Jackson Graham, Heather Graham, Sam Graham, Mr W.Graham, Mrs Graham, S. Graham, Dr Stuart Graham, Mrs Gant, David Grant, Neil Grant, Bill Gray, Bob Gray, G. Lloyd Gray, L. Green, Mrs J.T. Green, Robert & Alison Greenshields, Alan Greer, Neil & Corinna Gregory, David H. Greig, Mr A. Grieg, Pat Greig, John Grieve, Martin Grieve, Peter Griffith, Roger Griffith, Jinny Grimble, Prof N.R. Grist, Simon Grove, J. & A. Gudge, R. & M. Gulliver, Alastair H.Gunning, William Guthrie,

Irene Hackness, Dr D. L. Hadley, Mrs J. Hagley, K. Haining, Peter Hall, John B. Halliday, Mrs G. Hamblen, Mr K. Hamblin, Allister Hamilton, Andy Hamilton, Catherine S. Hamilton, Mrs. Hamilton, Janice Hampson, E. Geoff Hancock, Mr Hannah, Mr Hanniford-Hill, Bill Hansen, Graham Hardy, Peter Hardy, Mrs Jennifer R. Harkes, Anne Harper, M. Harper, J. Harrison, Mr Hartshorn, Mr M.C. Harvey, Mr. Hassan, Tom Hastings, J. Hastings, Mr D. Hawker, R.D. Hawkins, B. Hay, Mr J.B. Hay, Kenny Hay, David Hayes, Keith Heaven, Mrs C.R. Hedderwisk, Moira A. Hemmings, Mr Henderson, Roy Henderson, Mrs G.

Hendren, Dick Hendry, Iain Hendry, J. Henry, M.F.D. Henry, Cliff J. Henty, David Herd, Mrs J. Heron, Rebecca Herron, David Heyes, Mrs Higgins, Mr Robert Hill, Mrs J. Hillis, Stephen H. Hind, R. Hissett, Robbie Hitchcock, Peter Hogbin, Russel Hobson, Mr J. Hodgeson, Angus Hogg, R.H. Hogg, Nick Holding, A Holding, Jane Holdings, John Peter Holland, T. & D.M. Holland, Roger Holme, R. Hope, David Horsefield, Kathryn Horsepool, P. Horsley, Nick Hoskins, James How, John How, Doreen Howard, Jamie & William Howard, Charlie Howe, Drs M.A. & E.A. Howe, Mike Howes, Joan Howie, Ted Hoyle, D.C. Hulme, Dick Hunter, Mike Hunter, Duncan Hutt, James Hutton, Mrs. Hyland, Jimmy Hyslop,

Ross E. Imrie, Valerie Ingram, Graham Irving,

B. Jackson, G. Jackson, Laurie Jackson, Tim Jacobs, Eric Jamieson, Mr D.C. Jardine, David L. Jaszewski, Gail & Steven Jeffcoate, M. Jennings, Mrs M.E. Job, Julian Jocelyn, A. A. Johnson, C. Johnson, Dee Johnson, A. Johnston, Ian Johnston, Nancy Johnston, Mrs Sue Johnston, Barbara Joiner, Mrs A. Jones, Arthur Jones, J. Jones, Jane Jones, R.H. Jones, Susan Jones, Pat Jordan,

Russell Keggans, Jane Kelly, Christine Kemp, Louise Kendrick, Agnes Kennedy, Kirsty Kennedy, A. Kerr, Anne Kerr, A. Keys, Dr Mike Kibby, Mrs Patricia Kilgore, Lawrie King, Sarah King, Pete Kinnear, J. Kinross, Keith Kirk, Steve Kirkby, Mr A.W.Kirkland, Paul Kirkland, Mrs Kirkwood, Claudia Kitscke, Prof John Knowler, Bill Kydd, George Kyle, P.D. Kyle, Beryl V. Lamb, A. Lambert, Bob Lambie, Mrs Lamond, Ian Langford, H.W. Langridge, Margaret E. Langstaff, Mrs Joan A. Law, Mr A.J. Lawrence, Mr M. Laycock, Cairnie Le Cornu, Anne Leask, Stewart Leask, Mr R. Leishman, Simon Lennox, Robert Letham, G. Lewis, Sarah Lewis, Tony Lewis, Liz Leyden, Harriet Lindsay, Brian Lister,
G. Lister, Mark Litjens, Bill Little, C. Little, Vivien Little, Megs & John Little, Iain Livingston, Susan Livingstone, Anne

Lochhead, Christie Logan, Cordelia Logan, Norma Logan, P.V. Long, Fred & Sarah Longrigg, Alan Louden, Christopher J. Lowe, Dr Dorothy A. Lunt, Dr Lyall, J.B. Lyall, A. Lynn, Peter R. Lyon, Margaret Lyth,

Craig Macadam, K. Macaskill, Mrs McBain, Colin McBeath, Stewart McBirney, Alan McBride, Andrew McBride, Alice R. McCaig, Kevan McCallum, Frank McCann, John McCann, Norman McCann, Owen McCann, Scott Mcardle, Crear McCartney, Jim McCleary, James McColm, Linda McConaghie, Mrs E. McConnachie, Mrs McCranor, Mr McCue, Mrs McCulloch, Bob McCurley, Mr. McDermid, Mr. McDonald, A. Macdonald, Gillies Macdonald, Mrs E.J. MacDonald, Jean MacDonald, Dr M. MacDonald, Mrs Susan Macdougall, Helen McEachran, Alistair Macewan, Sharon McEwan, Mrs C. McFadyen, Duncan Macfadyen, Catherine I. McFadzean, Mrs Elizabeth McFadzean, Iain M. Macfarlane, Stuart Macfarlane, Wendy Macfarlane, Mrs J Macfarquhar, Catherine McFie, S McGhie, Mr McGill, Neil McGill, F. MacGillivray, Michael McGinnes, Marco McGinty, Lorraine McGlinchey, L. McGrath, Sandra McGreut, Andrew McGuire, Brenda McIntosh, Mrs E. M. McIntosh, Nicola Macintyre, Donald W. Mack, Mrs McKay, Anne Mackay, C.R. McKay, Donald McKay, Esme Mackay, F. & J. MacKay, Jessie Mackay, Mairi McKay, Helen McKechnie, Mrs Jane McKeen, Chris McKeown, Hildegard M. McKeown, John Mackerige, Mrs A. McKenzie, John McKenzie, John M Mackenzie, Neil D. G. Mackenzie, Dr A.H.T. Mackichan, Ann McKillop, Mrs McKinlay, Mrs Betsy S. McKinlay, John McKinnell, Morag Mackinnon, P. Mackintosh, Ronald McLaren, Sandra McLaughland, Mr. McLaughlin, Mrs Marlies Maclean, Sandra Maclean, Simon McLean, Mrs Margaret McLellan, L. Maclellan, L. M. MacLellan, Anne Macleod, Rona Macleod, J. McMahon, John McMillan, Robert A. McNaught, Hilary Macnaughton, A.K. McNeil, Dr. McNeill, John McOwat, Barbara McOwen, Andrew J.

McPartland, Mr McPhail, Christine Macpherson, Mrs Georgie Macrae, Liz McTeague, Irvine McVeagh, Donald N. McVean,

Peter Madden, Miss J. Maltman, Mrs Jane Manning, Mrs M. Manson, Yvonne Marjot, Richard Marks, Mrs W. Marrs, Mrs Martin, Angus Martin, Gail Martin, Grace Martin, Heather Martin, Henry Martin, Michael Martin, Mr W. Martin, Jenny Maskell, Mrs Jill Massey, Andrew Masterman, Mrs Elizabeth A.S. Mathie, Martin Matthews, J.L. Maxwell, Jimmy Maxwell, John Maxwell, M. Mayes, Richard & Barbara Mearns, Robert Mears, Forbes Meek, Mr V.C. Mella, David Mellor, Jamie & Morag Mellor, Dr J.T. Mercer, G. Mercer, Jo Mercer, Dr Jon Mercer, John B. Merler, D. Merrick, E. Middleton, Clair & Adam Millar, Jean Millar, Karen Miller, Keith Miller, Miss Abby Miller, Ronald H. Miller, Catherine Mills, Lesley Mills, Mr H. Milner, Mr D. Mitchel, Jean Mitchell, John Mitchell, Laurie Mitchell, Bruce Moglia, John Moir, Richard Moore, John R. Moran, Joanna R. Morgan, Sian Morgan, D.C. Morris, Catriona Morrison, Mrs P. Morton, Matthes Mosley, Harry Mottram, Ann Moule, N.P. Muddiman, Denis Muir, Jim Muir, Mr Munn, Mrs Munro, Mrs Linda Munro, Alastair D. Murdoch, Paula Murdoch, Douglas J. Murphy, C. Murray, Catrione Murray, Mrs V. Murray, Miss J. Muscott, Fiona Mutch,

K. Naylor, Mr A.R. Nelson, G. Newell, Miss B.J. Newman, Mr Niblo, Mrs Nicol, Mrs Gill Nisbet, Russell G Nisbet, Ronald C. Niven, Peter Norman, Mrs Pam Northcott, Mrs W. Norton, Bob & Moira Nuttall,

Isabel O'Brian, Malcolm A. Ogilvie, A.L. Ogilvy, John O'Keefe, P. Oliver, Carol Omand, Mr P. Ormerod, Brian Orr, Mr C.W. Oswald, Fiona Owens,

E. Page, R. Paget, Mark Palmer, Mrs L. Park, Laura Parker, Rob Parker, Liz Parsons, V. Partridge, Myra Pater, Mr A. Paterson, Frances Paterson, James W. Paterson, Mrs Maryen Paterson, Mrs Maureen Paterson, Joyce W. Paton, Karen Paton, J.

Patrick, Bill Patterson, David Patterson, Mr G. Pearson, William Peden, David Perry, Mrs A. Petrie, Miss Flora M. Petrie, Mrs C.A.Phillips, David Phillips, John Phillips, Sheila Philips, Mrs J.C. Pickett, David Pickett, Nick Picozzi, M. Pink, Karl Pipes, Mrs E. Pirrie, John Plackett, Mark Pollitt, Catherine Pollock, Robert K. Pollock, F.M. Ponten, Rebecca Porter, Rob & Alex Porter, Sarah Postlewaite, Robert Potter, Mr B. Pounder, Barry Prater, Tom Prescott, Ross Preston, Brigid Primrose, Linda Primrose, D.J. & W.M. Proudman, E. Pugh, Mr I. Purcell, Ian Purvis,

Georgia Quinn,

Mrs Radley, Alex Ramsay, Fiona Ramsay, M. Ramsay, Susan Ramsay, John Randall, Jim G Rankin, M. Neal Rankin, Tracy A. Rankin, H.D. Rankine, Mrs M.E. Rankine, P.J.G. Ransom, Dr Neil Ravenscroft, Edward S.P. Rawston, John Raymond, Roger Reason, Kelvin Reel, Mrs J. Rees, D.M. Reid, D.J. Remington, J.C. Render, L. Rennie, John Rhead, Mrs A. Richardson, Mike Richardson, Iain Richardson, Andy Riches, Gordon Riddle, Adrian Riley, Ken Ritchie, Bill Robb, Brain Roberts, Sue Roberts, Brian Robertson, Helen Robertson, Jan Robertson, Mr Alistair Robertson, Mrs Jean Robertson, Mrs M.E. Robertson, Neil Robertson, Barry & Jean Robinson, H. Robinson, Jeanne Robinson, M. Robinson, Martin Robinson, Mrs J. Rodger, Mrs Sarah Rodger, E. Rogerson, Chris Rollie, Mrs J. Rooney, Irving Rosmoor, Dr A. John Rostron, F. Rout, Mark Ruggeri, Isabel Rule, Mrs E.M. Russell, Sheila Russell, A. Rutherford, Steve Ryder, Adam Samson, Mr A.G. Sandeman, Peter Sanders, R. Sanders, G.P.S. Sargant, Mrs D.J. Savill, Bob Saville, Mrs S. Saxton, D G. Scherrer, A. Scott, Bill Scott, D. Scott, S. Scott, Miss Mhairi Scott, R.P. Scott, R. Scott, Ruaridh Scott, Tony Scott, V. Scott, W.M. Scott, Cath Scott, R. Alexa Seagrave, B.A. Seale, Jean Seaton, Mr N. Semple, Jim Shanks, Mrs Sheila Sharp, Clem Shaw, Mrs. Shaw, Geoff Shaw, M. Shearer, Mrs F. Shedden, Mr P.A. Sheehan, David Shenton, Geoff Shepard, Rachel Shipley,

Mrs Margaret Shotter, Bryan Simpson, Fraser S. Simpson, Mrs E. Simpson, Mrs Simpson, Mrs S.S. Sinclair, Mr R. Singleton, Laura Sivell, Brian Skillen, Esther Skillen, Allen Skinner, William Laird Sloan, Mr Verity Small, Alan Smith, Alexander G.M. Smith, Andrew Smith, Mrs Chris Smith Christina Smith, Frank J. Smith, Mr R.G. Smith, Liam Smith, M.S. Smith, Neil Smith, R.W.J. & E.M. Smith, Rosemary Smith, Graham H Smith, Tony Smith, Chris Smout, Bill Smylie, Mrs E. Snedden, John R. Snodin, Richard Soulsby, Derek & Jean Southall, Carol Southby, Richard Southwell, David Speed, Dr S. Spencer, Jeremy Spon, Dr David Spooner, E.F. Spragge, Clair Spray, Stuart Spray, Dr J.E.R. Squires, Mrs E. Stables, Eleanor Stafford, Chris Stamp, Peter Stannard, Margaret Stead, Mrs Steel, Alan Steel, G. Steven, John Steven, M. Stevens, Rebecca Stevens, Jon Stevenson, Ms Stevenson, J.K. Steward, Emma Stewart, Mr J.W. Stewart, M. Stewart, Isobel M. Stewart, Agnes Stewart, Mrs T. Stinson, Allan Mcg Stirling, Jane J. Stirling, Nigel Stone, Julie Stoneman, Ian Strachan, Mary Strachan, Mrs Helen Strachan, Mrs S. Strachan, M. Stuart, Ian M. Stubbs, Mrs E. Sturrock, Pete Summers, Dr A. Sumner, Richard Sutcliffe, Alison Sutcliffe, Christine Sutcliffe, Kirsty Sutherland, Mrs P.S. Swettenham,

T. Norman Tait, Celia Tanner, S. McD. Tanner, Helen Taylor, John Taylor, Mary Taylor, Sally Taylor, Mary O. Tebble, I.D. Teesdale, William A.C Telfer; Mrs C.P. Templeton, Mrs Terry, Andre E. Thiel, B. Thomson, Chris D. Thomas, Mrs Rosemary Thomas, B.H. Thompson, D. Thompson, Emma Thompson, Mrs Ruth Thompson, B.H. Thomson, Dr George Thomson, John Thomson, M. Thomson, Mrs Thomson, Ron Thomson, Dr J.E. Thorpe, Graham Thursby, Jim & Carol Timms, Elizabeth Tindal, Mr G. Tinkler, Mr G. Titchmarsh, Mr Todd, R.A. Toller, Elizabeth & John Tolson , Chris Tudhope,

Mrs Joanna Turle, Robin Turner, K. Tyson,

Mr P. Ullrich,

Alexander Van Beest,

E. Waddell, Jeff Waddell, Kevin Waite, Judy Wakeling, Mrs L. Waldie, June Waley, Andrew Walker, Felicity Walker, Graeme Walker, Laura Walker, Steven Walker, Mr Walker-Graham, Michael Richard Wall, George & Val Wallace, Ian John Waller, A. Heather Walshaw, Mr & Mrs J. Warburton, Martin Warren, Mr Waterhouse, J. Waterworth, A. Watson, Dr Eric R. Watson, Gordon R. Watson, Keith Watson, Mrs Joan Watson, Hugh Watson, Duncan M. Watt, Wendy Watson, S. Watts, Richard Weddle, J.R. Weeks, Margaret M. Weir, David & Ann Welham, P. Wells, Valerie Wells, Christine Welsh, Peter W.A. West, Fred Westcott, Val Weston, P.R. Wheeler, Tom Whilty, Anna White, George White, M. White, Susan White, A Whitehouse, J. Whitehouse, Susan Whitelaw, Mr Whitfield, Alastair Whyte, Mrs. F. & Miss G. Whyte, Miss C.J. Widdop, Bridget Wilcox, A.M. Wilding-White, Jeanette Wilkin, M.A. Wilkins, Judy Wilkinson, Andrew Will, Jonathan Willet, Margaret Williams, Dr Miles Williams, Pru Williams, Peter Williams, Mrs D.L. Willis, Nigel Willits, Mr J. Wills, Mr P. Wilmot, A. Wilson, Mr & Mrs C.D. Wilson, James Wilson, Jim & Val Wilson, Mrs Jessie G. Wilson, Mr M.J.L. Wilson, Mrs Margaret Wilson, Maureen & Kirsty Wilson, Mrs S. Wilson, J. Winn, Mrs C. Winton, Sue Wiseman, James Wolstencroft, David Eric Wood, E. Wood, Catherine G. Woodford, C.W. Wood-Gee, Andrew Woods, C. Woodward, Fred R. Woodward, Mrs C. Woolacott, Gordon Woolley, Peter Wormell, Elma Wrench, A.A. Wright, David Wright, James Wyllie, Nick Wynn, Andrew Wyper,

Lynn Yardley, Mrs Yarr, Dr M.R. Young, Ms Elizabeth Young, Stuart Young, Tom Young, Helen Younger, R.E. Youngman,

Bernard Zonfrillo.

Postscript – the future

THIS ATLAS provides an accurate baseline of information about the status of butterflies in South West Scotland. The next step is to target recording and monitor those species which are vulnerable and have shown a decline. In particular, more detailed information is needed to evaluate the status of the Dingy Skipper, Marsh Fritillary, Pearl-bordered Fritillary and Large Heath.

For some species further research is required to fully understand their life cycle. Is the Common Rock-rose the sole foodplant of the Northern Brown Argus? Does the Purple Hairstreak prefer Pedunculate Oak and is its distribution linked to that of ants? What are the reasons for the fluctuation in numbers of the Small Tortoiseshell? Is parasitism an important factor in controlling the numbers of Marsh Fritillary in South West Scotland? These are just a few questions that indicate that we still have much to learn about these beautiful insects and that further research is essential to assist conservation efforts.

Female Purple Hairstreak. This butterfly is associated with Oak woodland. Although it may have been overlooked it does appear to be absent from many Oak woodlands in South West Scotland, for unknown reasons